MW01289822

There She Goes

A guide to solo female travel:
How to stay safe, sane and solvent on the road

Katie Monk

Cover image: Averie Woodard / Unsplash

ISBN: 9781708817749

Disclaimer

This book is intended for reference purposes only. The author bears no responsibility for any consequences resulting from the use of information provided in this book. Please use all information at your own risk. Although every effort has been made to ensure factual accuracy, the author is not responsible for any outcome.

CONTENTS

"This is real. This life. We're really here... this is really happening." – Zadie Smith

Dedication

This book is dedicated to all the girls and women I've met on my travels. Gallivanting the globe on your own is no mean feat, and I salute anyone who has the courage to do so, especially females. I hope this book inspires women of all ages and backgrounds to get out there and explore this beautiful planet.

For every book sold, 10% of the profits will go to Womankind, a charity that aims to end violence and oppression against women and girls for good.

Chapter One

Introduction

I read an interesting but depressing statistic the other day that said each year, twice as many men go on holiday than women, and I thought, what the heck is that about? I mean, obviously everybody is different, and there are myriad reasons why one person might take a holiday and the next not, but why are women not taking a break? Do they have an invisible force holding them back? If so, what is that force? Why are women not *getting away*?

All these questions spun round my mind that night, and I got angry about all the possible answers. Of course, I could understand it to an extent. But also, I couldn't. And it upset me. A lot.

The world is a huge, wonderful place, yet so many women see and experience only a small portion of it. This is a tragedy and a travesty. Aside from the obvious financial issues, perhaps the reasons could be a mixture of safety, societal pressure, expectation, and domestic responsibilities. Who knows? Maybe they don't *want* to go anywhere. Maybe they want to stay at home. Maybe we hold ourselves back.

What became clear to me through my research is that girls and women face many more challenges if and when we do decide to do things on our own, much of which can't be seen or measured – or even articulated. This is key. A lot of what I want to touch on in this book is hard to articulate and quantify. But I'm going to try. Statistics are out there, sure, but I don't feel they paint a true picture of what's really going on here. Plus there are only so many things you can tally up and put on a spreadsheet. Sub-conscious conditioning, mental blocks and social forces generally aren't some of them. Nor is the feeling you get when you're travelling, feeling free and in the "flow" state, which is the payoff for all the hard work needed to get out the front door in the first place.

One of my biggest motivations for writing this book was because I spend a lot of time travelling on my own. I also like loitering with intent in the travel sections of bookshops, and seldom do I see anything aimed squarely at me. On a carefully curated table named Rucksack Reads at my local Waterstones, I counted 49 books – only four of which were written by women. Of course, there was no shortage of tomes penned by gnarly-faced men recounting tales of death-defying adventures in far-flung lands. But women talking about women's travel? Not so much.

Nor did I see a whole lot in the guidebook section that

spoke specifically to me. I found a couple of side notes and chapters, but not much more. Nothing about nuances, instincts, feelings, the addictive nature of having complete agency and freedom, warding off unwanted attention on a night train in India, getting your period in the African bush, or how to wild camp on a solo hike in Sweden. In fact, most guides seemed to be written very much from a male (or perhaps, non-gendered) perspective. If I saw anything about camping, road trips or cycle trips, I'd be left wondering if the information would apply to me – if I could recreate the trip myself and feel safe and happy. The answers were not forthcoming.

I saw similar gender biases in nearly all the other non-fiction categories I browsed that day. Many books were resolutely (and again, probably sub-consciously) filtered through a male lens, which is not only alienating, but an inaccurate portrayal of the world in which we live. Sweeping generalisations and omissions are being made about the experiences of half of the human race. And this isn't right. Not to mention the experiences of LGBTQ+ people and people of colour, who also face huge amounts of oppression, prejudice and discrimination.

Perhaps when it comes to travel, gender isn't considered an important enough topic, or even sub-category? Yet in my experience, the world is a vastly different place – to both live and travel in – if you're female, doubly so if you're on your own while you're at it. The female aspect is *everything*. I don't mean that women are less capable, less ambitious or less strong, far from it. In many ways, we're far stronger than men. We're capable of the most audacious experiences ever, and deserve to have them. It's just that, for the most part, the world responds to us differently, and in unique ways, and that proves a sticking point.

One thing's for sure, travelling alone is an entirely different experience from travelling as a couple, in a group, and as a man. Therefore it deserves proper representation and understanding. Of course, there are common threads that run through all of these (a crocodile doesn't care about your gender, nor does a tsunami or a stomach parasite or a landslide), but the solo female traveller will face a huge array of particular experiences all to herself, *as well as* all these other things.

When I try talk about all of this to guys, most have very little awareness of what the world feels like to the opposite sex. They're seldom aware of this difference because it's like the air they breathe. It's just how it is. The world is built and set up for men, but they don't realise it. Some even point-blank deny it, and insist (in the Western world, at least) that it's a level playing field. Yet nothing could be further from the truth. And when girls say they don't notice a difference, I think they've either been incredibly lucky (and I hope continue to be), or they haven't got out enough. I even once had an ex-boyfriend tell me, quite angrily, I may add, as I recounted a story about sexual harassment in my home town, that I should be grateful I don't live in the Middle East.

I think Caitlin Moran summed it up quite nicely in her book, *Moranifesto*, when she said the only real relatable equivalent would be for men to imagine living in a world populated by bears, and everywhere they go they might be attacked.

That's not to say there aren't any female travel writers – there are lots, and I've listed some of my favourites in the Resources section – it's just they're woefully outnumbered and underrepresented. One of my favourite books is *Women Travellers*, edited by Mary Morris, which includes essays and travelogues by some of the most famous female writers in history. The fact that these women travelled in the era they did is testament to their spirit and bravery (and sometimes foolhardiness).

Thankfully, more female travel writers are coming through. There's Cheryl Strayed and Elizabeth Gilbert (both of whom had their books turned into Hollywood films), Anna Hart, Bonita Norris and Kristin Newman. There's Sara Wheeler – who I heard speak at Stanford's bookshop in 2003, and who (along with my sister) inspired me to jet off to Peru, Chile and Argentina the following year. Finally, people I could relate to.

The blogosphere is also full of female travel influencers. There's Jennelle Eliana, Marina from Pam the Van (who now travels by motorbike), Oneika the Traveller, RayaWasHere, IAmAileen, As The Magpie Flies, Chelsea Kauai, Sorelle Amore, Melody Alisa... the list goes on... proving there's a huge appetite for solo female travel at the moment. On YouTube, 70 of the top 100 most-viewed videos in 2019 with "solo travel" in the title were uploaded by women.

In the wake of the Me Too movement, it seems we're finally on a roll. Amen for that.

I now meet so many women and girls gallivanting solo – of all ages, cultures, creeds and abilities. In fact, nowadays I probably meet more girls than guys – a trend that is growing by the day. According to WorldPackers.com, an average of 72% of American women like to travel alone, and 55% of travel searches in the UK at the moment are for solo female travel. And this isn't just single ladies, either. Last year, Lonely Planet reported that 60% of solo travellers were married or in a relationship. Quite how many of those were female, I'm not sure, but my guess is they couldn't have all been guys. I also meet my fair share of single mums on the road, too. Perhaps it's just travel literature and television that hasn't caught up yet.

So, if you *are* thinking about travelling, rest assured you'll be in good company. Female dorms are becoming more commonplace, helping us to feel safer and more connected, and where you quite often meet friends for life; the internet is rife with inspiration; and technology means planning and booking is a cinch.

My hope is that this book will inspire you and prepare you to join the club.

Chapter Two

My Travels

_____

"It's a dangerous business, Frodo, going out your door. You step onto the road, and if you don't keep your feet, there's no knowing where you might be swept off to." – J.R.R Tolkien

I didn't deliberately decide to travel alone, it just happened.

As a child I used to love taking myself off for long walks in the woods. We lived in quite a safe village, so I was allowed a great deal of freedom. I used to build dens, climb trees, and generally amuse myself outside for days on end, and I loved it. I've always been very content in my own company.

Then at the age of 16, I spent a summer looking after two very small children in the South of France. I didn't enjoy it, felt really isolated and lonely, and ended up coming home early. I'm a bit of a home body, truth be told, and it takes a great deal of effort for me to push myself out of my comfort zone. I knew that travel was a good thing – I just didn't take to it naturally.

To make matters worse, I then started getting panic attacks a lot, and often wouldn't leave the house. The thought of getting in a car would give me anxiety, let alone taking a train or plane. But flying to the other side of the world seemed so outrageous, it seemed my only cure.

So just after my 19th birthday, I bought a round-the-world ticket through a company called BUNAC. I didn't know anyone who'd ever done such a thing. This was before gap years were invented, and at the time, I didn't even think I'd be going to university anyway. Travel was not in my field of vision.

With BUNAC, I flew to Australia, via Bangkok. Bangkok in the Nineties was quite different from the small town in Wiltshire where I was from. I still remember the musty, humid smell, and the proliferation of bright yellow-gold. From there, we flew to Sydney, and myself and another girl buddied up and travelled around Australia picking up odd jobs in cafes and restaurants – we figured that was a good way to get fed.

The trip was a gamble, but it paid off. Spending so much time outdoors in nature, travelling vast landscapes, moving slowly, being around laid-back Aussies and their no-worries attitude was like therapy. There was also something about the sheer size of Australia, and its distance from home, that I needed. It was all reassuringly unfathomable.

This was pre-internet. Letters were sent to a service called Poste Restante, which held onto them until I was ready to have them forwarded every month or so, usually to a small town I knew I'd be passing through in a week's time. When I got there, I'd pick up my mail, bound together with elastic bands, and take myself off somewhere quiet to read each letter over and over again, crying and laughing at the stories, drawings and handwriting. It would take me a day or two to get back into the swing of things after that. Phoning home was rare – the cost of long-distance calls made from clapped-out old phone boxes in the Outback was a luxury I usually couldn't afford.

But the "letting go" element was a revelation. I don't know if I've experienced anything like it before or since, now we're all connected all the time. Every single thing I did that year took me way, way out of my comfort zone, and further and further into the realm of freedom. Out of my head and into my body, in short.

After about six months, myself and the girl I was travelling with parted ways. I think we'd hung onto each other for moral support as we were both so young (she was just 18). But the time had come to go it alone. It was a really strange feeling at first, but I think it was the making of me. And I've come to love my solo travels and my little mini-breaks. They feel like precious gifts to myself.

I was still 19 when I landed back in the UK, but I may as well have been 39 or 49. My mind and nervous system were completely renewed. I wasn't terrified anymore. A new world had been opened up to me.

Since then I've made travel my mission. I've been to countless countries on my own, sometimes for days, weeks and months. I've lived in many different places. I've had massive highs and massive lows. But even the "bad days" make good stories in the end. I wouldn't change any of it. I've hiked around the Himalayas, had leeches crawl inside my ears in the rainforest in Laos, been charged by a rhino in Zimbabwe and played polo with gauchos in Argentina. I've learned salsa in Cuba, tango in Buenos Aires, and massage in Thailand.

Travel has been my school, my saviour and my safety valve. It's been my oxygen in a very stuffy world. Simply put, I cannot imagine ever living without it. It has allowed me, and continues to allow me, to spend valuable time with myself. To cross paths with the most incredible souls; to do what I want, when I want, how I want (within reason); take precious, soul-searching, healing time; to challenge myself; try new things; be away from the crippling constraints and judgements of polite society; to practice my photography; read books; write books; listen to music and watch films alone; enjoy much-needed thinking time, writing time, painting time, work-out-what-I-want-in-life time; and any number of activities that don't require anybody else's presence or input. Best of all, it makes me feel truly alive.

Chapter Three

Finding the courage to go

_____

"Choose courage over comfort, 'cos you can't have both." – Brené Brown, author and researcher

If you've ever wanted to know what magic feels like, just do some spontaneous travel. On good days it's like being in the "flow state", the creative state, the most alive state of all.

Sure, you could travel in a pre-planned intellectual way, and often this is a good way to start, if you're not sure what to do, or time is of the essence. But I highly recommend leaving some room for improvisation, because that's when things get interesting. Travelling in this way is like having a conversation with life. You don't come at it from a head space, but rather an intuitive place. What is being said here? Do I like it? Do I stay or leave? What do I feel like doing? What's my gut telling me? And if you're brave enough to follow the answers, that's where the gold lies. Many of the best trips I've taken were about acting on impulse, letting go, shedding some of the old identity, and allowing the space and possibility for something unexpected to unfold.

The brain is hardwired to keep us safe. It's not hardwired to make us happy, or challenge us. We have to do this ourselves. Most things we do will keep us in our comfort zone. If we push ourselves, we may immediately start to feel uneasy, because the warning bells are telling us to get back where we belong, where the brain thinks we'll be OK. This can be back home, school, work, a relationship, old friendships, the town you live in, anything. The comfort zone can be both literal and figurative.

We have to disrupt our own lives – rarely will someone do it for us.

Time also expands when you go away, especially if you have the discipline to be semi-unplugged. Anyone who's ever been travelling will tell you how much they did while they were gone, and how it felt like they'd been away much longer than they actually had. A day can last a week because of the amount of interactions and experiences that occur. I like to think of it as a way to extend life. Since space-time is elastic, and difference and newness effectively elongate it, our lives seem longer, fuller, richer. It's one of the best life hacks I know. Contrast this with time spent at home going through the motions, where the days, months and years drift by.

It's only when we do something new that our conscious "thinking" brain has to sit up and take notice. Travel is full of newness. Away from familiarity, we have to take in thousands of new pieces of information each second and make some kind of sense of it. We're walking through grass that hasn't been walked through yet. It feels challenging, tough, but incredibly rewarding. We're learning something new. We will remember this day. Our beliefs are challenged. Our habits are changed. New neural pathways are formed, and when we look back on our life, chances are it's these times – these breaks from the norm – that will stand out in our mind. The rest, as they say, is leaf litter.

Chapter Four

Why do women travel solo?

_____

"Some women choose to follow men, and some women choose to follow their dreams. If you're wondering which way to go, remember that your career will never wake up and tell you it doesn't love you anymore." – Lady Gaga

There are myriad reasons why women travel on their own. For some, it's not even a decision. Perhaps they're single. Perhaps their partner or friends can't or don't want to come with them, for whatever reason, so they either go on their own or don't go away at all. Maybe there are financial constraints or time constraints or a clash in desirable destinations.

Other women simply prefer it. They're happy in their own skin, and enjoy the freedom and independence that solo travel brings. They like not having to answer to anyone. If they feel like lying in bed all day, they can. If they feel like leaving, they leave. They're not answerable to anyone. Plus, not all company is created equal. Often it's better to actually *be* alone than with someone who makes you *feel* alone.

Many women start off travelling solo due to circumstances, then end up continuing out of choice. The more you do it, the more you fall in love with it, then it becomes really hard to share a trip with someone else.

Travelling alone can be daunting, yes, but it can also be incredibly liberating and thoroughly enjoyable. I'm not against travelling with others – this can also be truly wonderful – it's just that it's a very different experience. Especially travelling with a man because nearly everywhere you go, he is the one who people automatically address, not you, and that can make you feel invisible, belittled and unimportant. So it's quite nice being the one in charge, the one calling the shots.

Solo travel isn't just a young person's game, either. In a US study from July 2017, 79% of older female respondents (and 93% of men) said the idea of having to travel solo didn't stop them from taking trips[1] They'd get out there regardless, and see the world while there's still time.

On a recent trip to Portugal, I was amazed how many women over 60 I met who were backpacking around. Some had just retired and were now taking full advantage

---

[1] https://www.statista.com/statistics/377082/hesitance-to-travel-alone-among-older-generations-us/

of their newfound freedom; others had lost partners; some had grown-up children and grandchildren and weren't needed at home as much any more. One Texan lady I met was taking a break from working in a pop-up Halloween shop in Austin to drive around Portugal learning about cork; another had just hiked the Camino de Santiago and was on her way to Scotland to tackle the West Highland Way; a German lady I met was taking time out of her business as a massage therapist in order to recharge her own batteries after always helping others recharge theirs. Yet another had travelled from Argentina after retiring, and didn't speak a word of English. It gladdened my heart to meet them all – and in hostels too! Most were sleeping in dorms, and all were enjoying the freedom and camaraderie that solo travel brings.

In the UK, the YHA hostels tend to attract an older crowd, who generally go to bed early and rise early. Some of them also attract families and school groups, so call ahead if you don't wish to be surrounded by kids. But otherwise, generally mid-week is quieter, and a good bet if you're after some peace and quiet and a good night's sleep. The same goes for the international HI hostel network. I've found these to attract an older demographic, so if this is you, they're a great place to meet people of a similar age. Annual memberships are available for both, and give you discounts and benefits.

Chapter Five
Am I going to be happy?

———————

"One can only really travel if one lets oneself go and takes what every place brings without trying to turn it into a healthy private pattern of one's own, and I suppose that is the difference between travel and tourism."
– Freya Stark, travel writer and explorer

I've never really been drawn to holidays in the traditional sense. They feel like replacing one bubble with another. What I love about solo travel is the way you can get under the skin of a place in a very real and raw way. The times I've spent travelling alone have been like slices of pure joy, gaps among the clouds, being plugged into the mains. Some people think of travel as running away from life; but I think of it as running towards. It's as close to pure reality as it's possible to get in the 21st century. I also believe that travel is part of our human nature, and nomadic life is part of our DNA. In an era where many of us feel stagnant, lost, lonely and disconnected, it provides a ready injection of purpose, community and connection.

It's also more important than ever, as it affords you a window into how other people live, and that in turn, helps to dissolve boundaries, us-and-them mentalities, stereotypes and prejudice. Travel gives you perspective, and that definitely adds to the net amount of happiness on the planet – or perhaps just gratitude and tolerance.

So will you be happy? Yes, yes and yes! Will it be easy? No! Will bad things happen? Potentially! But you'll get through it. And you'll come out the other side knowing first-hand a joy that is so pure, so natural, you'll wonder how you ever lived without it. This is why we keep going back for more. It's a transcendental experience, like having a key to a magic kingdom. .

There will be ups and downs, absolutely. One day you might be missing home, lose your passport, get the worst food poisoning ever, and be sharing a room with a walrus with a head cold; the next you'll be swimming in a crystal-clear waters, having deep-and-meaningfuls with a total stranger and feeling totally at one with the world. No two days are the same – that is the beauty of all this.

Luckily the good days will outweigh the bad. And if not, you can always come home. Nobody is making you stay in an unhappy place feeling miserable. Coming home is ALWAYS an option (side note: this has happened to me once in 30 years). When you realise you always have a choice, you can relax a little and go with the flow.

It takes a while to let go of life as you know it – a bit like letting go of the hand rail at the ice rink, but once you do, and you glide around the world, you won't actually want to come home.

Letting go does require discipline, however, as it's so easy to still be connected to home in a way that doesn't truly allow you to be free and experience the pure joy of travel that I'm referring to. You can be Whatsapping friends and family all day long, positing your pictures on Instagram, and checking emails the whole time, if you want. But try and resist this – try and really be there in the moment, not in a thousand other virtual places. Because this is where the magic lies.

I still get really nervous before going anywhere. But I realise that's just my brain's in-built mechanism to keep me safe (ie, stuck in my comfort zone). Once I'm on the plane or at my destination, all thoughts of life beforehand disappear. All the planning, packing and sleepless nights become totally worth it. It takes mountains of effort and courage, but the rewards are immense. Even though I love travel, and have been to many places alone, it still requires a monumental amount of courage for me to do it. That never changes or gets easier. But much of the gold in life comes from pushing through these mental barriers and coming out the other side. Travel is no exception.

Travel is one of the best things you can do for yourself, and lucky for us, we're living in an age where it's all completely possible.

Chapter Six

Start Small

"So here's your life
We'll find our way
We're sailing blind
But it's certain nothing's certain.

I don't mind
I get the feeling
You'll be fine
I still believe that
In this world
We've got to find the time
For the life of Riley."

The Life of Riley by the Lightning Seeds

None of this has to involve huge amounts of sacrifice or cost. Travel isn't an all-or-nothing game. You don't need to give up your day job, flog all your belongings on eBay and spend a fortune on a long-distance plane ticket. You can travel at the weekends and during your annual leave, you can travel closer to home, within your budget, and within your comfort zone, then build it up slowly. The most important thing is to find your own way to get out there.

If the idea of travelling to another country on your own scares the living daylights out of you, then reel it in and travel more locally. Heck, you could even "travel" in your home town. Hang out wherever the tourists hang out – you'll soon feel like you're in a different place entirely. Book a night in a hostel, hotel or B&B. Whatever gets you out of your comfort zone until you feel ready to do this on a bigger scale.

One thing I will say, however, is that sometimes going big can sometimes be easier than staying small – sort of shock tactics, if you will (see my Australia adventure). When you go all in, there's no safety net, and it's amazing how much resourcefulness you can muster. But if all that really does send you into a blind panic, take it slow. This is your life, after all.

Don't forget there are plenty of travel companies for people who don't want to travel on their own. If you don't feel ready to take the plunge, have a look at Intrepid, Wild Frontiers, Explore and Exodus – all of which offer excellent group tours for those who don't want to travel alone. You could always travel solo afterwards, thus getting the best of both worlds. There are also more niche sites to check out, such as Health & Fitness Travel, Chicks on Waves and Responsible Travel. I've outlined some more in the Resources chapter at the end of this book.

Chapter Seven

Challenges of travelling solo as a female

────────────────

- Traveling alone is like being at the coalface of life with a spotlight on you. All manner of things will happen to you, and there is no buffer between you and the world. You'll be absorbing it all and dealing with it all by yourself, every day. You have to be up for this.

- You will often be the centre of attention. You'll be whistled at, told to smile by complete strangers, asked where you're from a thousand times a day, get approached in the street, in cafes, galleries and museums, sometimes with innocence and inquisitiveness, sometimes hostility, sometimes a mixture of all of these. You might be groped, followed, stared at, cat-called, asked personal questions and proposed to.

- When people are rude to you, or try to rip you off, or patronise you, bully you or scare you – and they will – you won't have anyone to turn around to and say, "What the hell was *that* about?!" You have to suck it up, shrug it off, and try and get on with your day. This can be very hard, especially if you're a sensitive soul.

- As well as being highly conspicuous, you can also be completely invisible. The solitary female can get swamped by a group of people who won't notice her, she can get bumped into countless times and not served at a bar or table because she's not seen, or the staff assume you're waiting for someone. She can end up being the free counselling service to all and sundry, who take her politeness as an invitation to unburden themselves for hours on end. She can be the automatic childcarer when adults have had enough of their kids, and allow them to bother her, clamber all over her and draw on her arms in crayon. It's assumed that she loves all children and animals, all of the time.

- Dining alone can often be a cue for waiting staff to chat you up or moan about their job, or misguided families and couples to invite you to join them because they feel sorry for you, or worse, give you pitying looks then talk about you as if you're not there. If you're a self-respecting adult, and want to be left alone in peace, this can be maddening.

- You are responsible for everything that happens on your trip, and this can be very tiring and stressful.
- You have to make all the decisions, and they're not always easy ones to make.
- There's nobody around who knows you well, and who you don't have to explain yourself to. It can sometimes feel like nobody understands you.
- Travel isn't comfortable. In fact, it's very often uncomfortable. That's the whole point.
- When you get sick, and you will, you have to look after yourself, and that is really tough.
- People will tell you you're "very brave" and to "be careful" a lot. And that can get patronising and annoying.
- It can get lonely.
- It can feel hugely awkward, especially during mealtimes in busy places if there are lots of couples and families around. There is a certain element of shame attached to being a solo woman. Why are you not with someone? What is wrong with you?
- Coming home is absolute hell. You don't know who you are anymore, people often don't know how to relate to you, and you them. It can be very

hard reintegrating into your old life and friendships. Coming home is much harder than leaving. Nobody will tell you that.

- It can be much more expensive travelling solo than with someone else. This is extremely annoying seeing as you only earn one-person's wages, yet two people earning two-people's wages pay half.
- There is no safety net, so it's pretty scary.
- There is no security.
- There is nobody to fall back on when the chips are down.
- In many places, being alone still feels like a subversive act.

Chapter Eight

Benefits of travelling solo as a female

"I like not knowing where I'm going."
– Tilda Swinton, British actress.

- It's incredibly rewarding planning a trip, and seeing it through on your own – there's a real sense of achievement involved. And to say you grow and learn as a person is an understatement.
- It's easier to meet people when alone. Not only are you more approachable, you're more open to talking to others. When you're with a friend or partner, you travel in a bubble. Your focus is in an entirely different place.
- You absorb and interact with your environment a lot more. There's no place to hide.
- When you're alone, people take you at face value as an individual, rather than as part of a couple or group. They see *you*. Not the blended half-of-someone-else version.
- You can hear, and develop, your instincts. And you're more likely to follow them and stay safe or

get out of your comfort zone.

- You can think for yourself and avoid the terrible affliction known as group-think (or couple-think).
- As a female, people tend to trust you more. You're less of a threat, so you get invited into people's homes, children will laugh and play with you, people will open up and talk to you – you get to learn about people's lives and hear incredible stories.
- You make tons of new friends.
- You can also be alone if you want and enjoy some solitude.
- You become confident, responsible, self-sufficient and capable.
- You become more broad-minded and tolerant. You meet people who don't necessarily adhere to your own world view, and that is a challenge. You learn that the world is made up of lots of different kinds of people, doing lots of different things, with different ways of thinking and doing things.
- Nobody knows your back-story, so you can be whoever you want, and share as much information as you feel like.
- Sometimes it can actually be safer.
- You can go with the flow. You don't have to

explain yourself or have a plan.

- You don't have to compromise.
- You can come and go as you please. You can change your mind if you want.
- You don't have to worry about someone else's safety and whereabouts.
- If you're open to it, amazing things will happen that you least expect. Things that you'll tell your grandchildren about that will make their eyes stand on stalks.
- You'll experience mind-boggling coincidences.
- You'll find your place in the world.
- You have the time to really find out what you want out of life and what makes you happy.
- You'll feel empowered.
- You can learn new skills.
- You can find your tribe.
- You'll feel free.
- You'll feel truly alive.
- You'll experience pure joy.
- You'll experience magic.

Warning: Travelling alone can lead to FREEDOM

Chapter Nine

Some great places to travel to on your own

"Whatever you're meant to do, do it now.
The conditions are always impossible."
– Doris Lessing,
British-Zimbabwean novelist

1. Japan
2. Portugal
3. Spain
4. Slovenia
5. Canada
6. Australia
7. New Zealand
8. Finland
9. Uruguay
10. Chile
11. Bali
12. Berlin
13. Amsterdam
14. Nepal

15. Sweden
16. South Africa
17. Peru
18. Cambodia
19. Switzerland
20. Austria
21. Iceland
22. Thailand

Some top places to stay

1. Tag Boutique Hostel, Lagos, Portugal

2. Ecomama Hostel, Amsterdam, Netherlands

3. For You Hostel, Seville, Spain

4. The Independente Hostel, Lisbon, Portugal

5. Home Lisbon Hostel, Lisbon, Portugal

6. The Limelight Hostel, Kyoto, Japan

7. Nui Hostel and Lounge, Tokyo, Japan

8. Wild Spirit Backpackers, Nature's Valley, South Africa

9. Once in Cape Town, Cape Town, South Africa

10. The Sanctuary, Koh Phangan, Thailand

11. The House of Sandeman, Porto, Portugal

12. Sophie's Hostel, Prague, Czech Republic

13. CoDE Pod Hostel, Edinburgh

Chapter Ten

What will other people think of me?

───────────────

**"Be alone – that is the secret of invention.
Be alone – that is where ideas are born."
– Nikola Tesla**

What I want to say here is, "Who cares?" but I know that other people's opinions can, and do matter. Will I be judged? Pitied? Envied? Told I'm crazy? Potentially yes to all of these things. Telling your friends and family about your plans can bring out a wide range of responses and opinions, solicited or otherwise. Then there are myriad reactions from the people you meet on the road.

In most places, you'll be welcomed and looked after. You might also be a magnet for conversation and attention. This can be good and bad, depending on the circumstances and location, which I'll discuss later. But you *will be a magnet*. Even in the 21st-century, a woman travelling alone is regarded with a mixture of suspicion, respect, concern, admiration, curiosity, shock, hostility, caution, wonder and confusion – sometimes all in one hour, by both males and females, old and young, by locals and fellow travellers. Some people will express their views openly to you, others will keep it to themselves but you can tell what they're thinking.

And not just in the countries you might think, either.

I met a girl recently who was hiking the Thames Path in the UK, on her way to its source. We bumped into each other one sunny Sunday while I was swimming in the river, and she stopped to rest and chat. I asked if she ever gets scared walking on her own, especially in the countryside. She said no, not really, only when the trees form a canopy overhead and she can't see anyone else around. I asked if she ever felt self-conscious, or wondered what others thought of her, and she told me a story about one afternoon when she was lying on the grass gazing up at the clouds, minding her own business. She'd been there a good while, and it was getting late, when a lady walking a dog stopped and began staring at her. The lady didn't say anything, and didn't get too close, but it made this girl feel really uneasy, and somehow ashamed of being alone, gazing up at the sky. She ended up getting up and walking off because she felt so uncomfortable. She said it was a huge tragedy that she couldn't just be left alone in peace to gaze up at the sky. In many places, relaxing on your own as a woman is tantamount to fixing a huge neon sign to your head that says: "I'm lonely, available, interested and weird. Come and bother me or stare at me".

Bottom line is, if you're going to do this, you need to be prepared for other people's looks, opinions and reactions, and try not to take them to heart. It's hard, I know. But, quite honestly, as long as you're not harming or offending anyone, and they're not harming or offending you, it's none of anyone's business what you do. After all, it's taken you a lot of guts to get out there, so don't let anyone ruin it. You gaze up at the sky all you want.

Chapter Eleven

Some tips on being alone

"To fall is to understand the universe."
– Author unknown

It can feel a bit strange going away on your own at first. I know lots of people who travelled alone once and didn't like it, and that's fair enough. But I think solo travel doesn't always reward you the first time around. It's a skill like any other, and takes time to practice, like riding a bike. There are a few wobbles to begin with, then you're off. And there's no feeling like it – you'll be hooked.

I've found various techniques to help reduce any feelings of awkwardness, paranoia, loneliness and self-consciousness.

1. Have one or two key things planned for the day ahead.
2. Make an effort to talk to people, even if you don't necessarily feel like it, and ask them about themselves. Listen to the answers – they might surprise you. This is what travel is all about.

Hostels and coffee shops are great places for striking up conversation.

3. Before you travel, load up your phone with your favourite music and podcasts, in case you can't get any internet on the road. I've made a list of a few of my favourites in the Resources section. Though be mindful of "zoning out" of the world around you and living in a bubble.

4. When dining alone, carry a good book/eReader/tablet, magazine or newspaper (ideally a local one) to enjoy while you eat. You could also write postcards or your journal. All these things can keep you company and make you feel less self-conscious or weird. Though be prepared to ditch them in favour of good ol' conversation, people-watching and food enjoyment. Food really is far tastier when you can actually savour it. Try eating at the bar, if you'd like to feel less awkward or have a fleet of ready-made companions. Sushi bars, window seats, banquettes and even coffee shops are good bets. Or if you prefer to dine alone (and who can blame you), eat a bit earlier or later to beat the rush. My personal favourite is to have a proper meal at lunchtime, when it's less cringy, then grab a snack or something lighter later on. Also, it's a good idea

to dress modestly, so others don't think you're waiting for a date. Unless, of course, you're open to offers.

5. Although it can be very comforting to constantly chat to friends and family, if your mind is still "at home", so to speak, you won't notice many of the people and opportunities surrounding you. For example, you might be sitting in a cafe Whatsapping your mum when the person at the next table could turn out to be the love of your life or your new best friend or share some fascinating insights that you never would hear from anyone else. I'm not saying never use your phone, that would be crazy, but try to not let technology take you away from the reason you're travelling in the first place, otherwise it seems like a waste. Sometimes loneliness and awkwardness can lead to incredible things if you're able to ride them out and see where they take you.

Chapter Twelve

Meeting people

**"Knowledge, to enlighten and free the mind from clinging deadening prejudices
– a wider circle of sympathy with our fellow-creatures – these are the uses of travel."
– Mary Shelley, English novelist**

Just because you decided to get on a plane on your own, doesn't mean you have to be alone forever. You might not always have the choice – circumstances may dictate otherwise – but as a general rule, the great thing about solo travel is you can be alone when you feel like it, and be around others when you don't. And you can change your mind at any point.

Meeting people is like real-live alchemy. You go to a new place and the deck gets shuffled and you never know which hand you'll be dealt. It never stops blowing my mind how I've met people and how our paths might never have crossed. The fact I met *that* particular person in *that* place at *that* time, when the next day they (or I) would have been elsewhere... That's crazy talk!

One thing I've learned is that travel is less about the place, and more about the people. You can be in paradise but be miserable, and in a hell hole and be blissfully happy. Most of it is down to the company you keep.

It can sometimes feel a bit awkward chatting to someone you don't know, especially if you're British. But just remember other people are probably feeling the same way. Asking them where they're from, where they've just been and where they're going is the usual opening gambit, so start with that and see where the conversation takes you. People love being asked about themselves, as well as for advice, so you could ask for a recommendation for a hostel, place to eat, route, etc (this can be anything – it doesn't have to be a genuine request), then get chatting from there. This one tactic alone has opened up *tons* of new friendships in my life. It takes a bit of practice but then it becomes second nature, and it's a valuable life skill to have. You could also compliment someone on something, and strike up a conversation from there.

For example, I met my friend Cathy in a tiny restaurant in a tiny village in the north of Laos (just before the leech incident). I saw she was sat on her own, and I just went up to her and asked if she knew of any hiking companies she could recommend. We got chatting, and met up again in Cambodia a few weeks later. A year after that, she moved to my home town to become an occupational therapist. That was 11 years ago, and we're still good friends to this day.

The travel community is actually one big family, and once you start travelling, you'll soon become a part of it. And I'm pretty sure that most of the friends I've made would have totally passed me by had I been in a bubble with someone else. But because I was alone, I made the effort to get to know these people, and I was also then able to spend time with them without feeling guilty about neglecting someone else.

If you want to meet travel buddies before you leave home, there are lots of meet-up groups and forums, such as MeetUp, Couchsurfing and InterNations – or groups such as Travel Advice by Travel Bloggers, The Solo Female Traveler Network, Ultimate Travel Group, Girls Love Travel, Travelettes and Girls Vs Globe.

You could also ask friends on social media if they have friends or contacts in the place you're visiting. This has been a lifesaver for me on many occasions. Even just posting a picture of where you are can often elicit a raft of messages from friends and contacts who either happen to be in the same place, or know someone who is.

I once had my purse stolen when I landed in Newark airport on my way to New York, so I sent a message to my friends on Facebook to tell them of my plight. Within an hour, a friend of a friend who lived in Queens offered me a bed for the night, so I went there. She turned out to be a gem of a person, and had just got back from location scouting for the film *Wild*, with Reese Witherspoon. I'd not heard of that story before, but I was about to go hiking on the Appalachian Trail, so this girl lent me her copy of *Wild* to read while I was doing it. I don't believe in coincidences, I believe everything happens for a reason, and everyone comes into our lives at the right time. This was just one example of such a meeting.

Another tip is to join a walking tour – many hostels offer free ones, even if you're not staying there yourself. I also like to take a yoga class. And if I'm in a town or city that has a Sofar Sounds gig, I'll sign up to one of those. I always meet tons of new people that way.

Chapter Thirteen

Getting there and around

_____

"Certainly, travel is more than the seeing of sights; it is a change that goes on, deep and permanent, in the ideas of living." – Miriam Beard, American historian and archivist

There are many ways you can travel affordably and safely around the world. Here are some of the best.

Booking Flights

1. Kiwi.com (my personal favourite)

2. Skyscanner.net

3. Kayak.com / Kayak.co.uk

4. Momondo.com / Momondo.co.uk

I use all these to cross-reference prices. I also check the airline's website to see if I can find the same flight cheaper there. If not, I'll book through whichever booking site or search engine had the best price. Remember to clear your cache and cookies in between checking prices, and use a browser such as Duck Duck Go or Brave. Booking engines track your searches, and often raise their prices the more you're keeping an eye on a flight. Use both your phone and your laptop to see if the prices differ before booking.

You can also sign up to newsletters such as Secret Flying and Jack's Flight Club, which have regular deals on flights, and will inform you via email if there's a promotion or an 'error fare' on, which can mean bargain-basement tickets.

Travelling by bus and coach

Megabus, Greyhound, Bolt Bus, Snap and National Express offer comfortable, affordable coach journeys, if booked in advance. My favourite is Megabus because the coaches are usually very new and well-equipped and also come with sockets and free wifi (if you can get that working on National Express, then you've struck gold).

In South Africa, there's a brilliant hop-on-hop-off

backpacker service called Baz Bus, which will drop you right at your hostel door – a real blessing in countries that you may not feel 100% safe in. Similar services exist in Australia (Oz Experience) and New Zealand (Kiwi Experience).

Travelling by train

Train travel is a great way to see a country (or crossing multiple countries). Once you're on board you can sit back and relax, without having to worry about traffic or navigation. Most countries have at least a skeleton rail network, though many have an impressive selection that can take you to even the smallest towns.

My first port of call for booking international trains is The Man in Seat 61 (www.seat61.com). Run by the British rail enthusiast, Mark Smith, it's the best resource for all things rail related, and includes detailed information on timetables, seating arrangements and even dining cars, with links to the correct portal for booking tickets.

Rail Europe (www.raileurope.com) is a good resource for planning and booking trains within Europe. If you're yet to turn 18, the EU Parliament has begun giving away Interrail tickets to EU citizens on their 18th birthday in a bid to encourage young people to discover the countries and cultures within Europe. What a fabulous idea. We need more cultural initiatives like that to ward off rampant nationalism and xenophobia. Not all teenagers get the chance to travel, but perhaps if they did, it would foster a more tolerant, respectful society.

If you're travelling within the UK, check out Virgin Trains (www.virgintrains.co.uk) for cheap deals. They cover the myriad rail networks in the UK and you can buy any journey through them and not pay a booking fee. You simply collect your tickets at most UK mainline stations (not just the one you're departing from).

Also in the UK, because we have such a ridiculously complex ticketing system, you can legally split your tickets, which means buying separate tickets for the same journey (without getting off the train). This can often work out cheaper than buying one through-ticket. To check on any potential savings, head to Split Your Ticket (www.splityourticket.co.uk) or Split Ticketing (www.splitticketing.com). If there is a saving, you can book directly on the Virgin Trains website, as above, and collect them all in one go.

In the US, I've used Amtrak (www.amtrak.com) a lot and really enjoy it. It's really easy to book your journey online, and download the tickets onto your phone. They have many long-distance routes, and it's a great way to see such a huge country. Even the names, such as the California Zephyr and the Texas Eagle, make me want to jump aboard right away!

Sleeper trains can be a great way to cover long distances – though, as with all modes of public transport, it's wise to take precautions. Personally I like to book my seat or sleeper carriage in advance so I'm guaranteed a place to relax (in the UK this is particularly important as many of the trains are overcrowded). In Portugal, you can get a seat in a first-class carriage for a few euros more. In countries like India I would advise upgrading so you feel safer. There are also sometimes designated carriages for women, which is a no-brainer. Dress very conservatively, and carry a pin to poke any stray hands.

In South Africa, I've taken the Shosholoza Meyl from Johannesburg to Cape Town on my own – a journey that took two nights and three days and cost £25 (www.shosholozameyl.co.za). I felt completely safe, and loved waking up to see zebras outside my window. And what nicer way to approach Cape Town than from the desert of the Karoo that slowly transforms into the mountains and vineyards of the Cape. For a more upmarket version, there's the five-star Rovos Rail (www.rovos.com) and the Blue Train (www.bluetrain.co.za).

Thailand has a good rail network, and you can book a basic bed for a very reasonable cost. The staff simply come around in the evening and make up the seats into beds, then you pull a curtain round and go to sleep. Make sure you book an upper bunk so you get a fan to keep you cool. The non-AC trains can get pretty sticky. And if you're travelling long distance by day, don't take a window seat. I did this once and inhaled diesel fumes for eight hours straight, and ended up looking like Oliver Twist. My lungs took about a month to recover.

And then, of course, you have the Trans-Siberian... Could there be a more adventurous and romantic way to see the world?

Chapter Fourteen

Where to stay

_____

"To awaken quite alone in a strange town is one of the pleasantest sensations in the world."
– Freya Stark, British explorer and travel writer

Now your flights and/or trains are booked, your next task is to work out where to stay. Some people like to have every night of their trip accounted for, but personally, I like to leave things much more open, and only book my first couple of nights then work out the rest as I go. I really don't like planning, and much prefer to be spontaneous, seeing how things pan out, who I meet, how I feel, etc. This for me is the joy of travel – letting it all unravel rather than micromanaging everything. Otherwise it just feels like an extension of life at home. If you rush around ticking places off a list there's no room for magic to happen. You're travelling, yes, but not in the real sense of the word. For me, the whole point is to experience a different way of living – to drop down a few gears and to listen to what life is telling me.

I recommend booking a private room in a hostel for

your first three nights. You will need that time to rest after your flight, get your bearings and generally acclimatise. Then you can either move into a dorm in the same hostel, remain in the private room, or book somewhere else. Hostels are a great place to make friends, get tips on places to go, plus have a safe and welcoming "home" to come back to (and often a a place to cook and do laundry, too).

Personally I prefer hostels to hotels or B&Bs because you're surrounded by likeminded people, and there's an instant social circle and often communal activities. But if you're not staying in a hostel, you can meet people in coffee shops, bars, buses, trains, on hikes, whilst volunteering, any number of ways. You could also join a walking tour or day trip – these are a great way to meet fellow travellers.

These days there are so many incredible hostels out there that you could travel for years and not experience all of them.

My particular highlights have been in Japan, Portugal, Germany, Australia and South Africa. In these countries, they're more like upmarket boutique hotels than hostels, and I've had some of the best times of my life there. Hostels are like ready-made holidays for the solo traveller. All you really need is a flight and a hostel and you're set. Have a look at the book *The Grand Hostels* by

Kash Bhattacharya for inspiration.

Please don't feel that age is a barrier to staying in a hostel. I meet women of all ages, and these days so many places offer female-only dorms. Even five years ago, this wasn't all that popular. Unsurprisingly they're nearly always fully booked – so bear this in mind when making your reservations. Many hostels also charge a premium for female dorms – something I don't agree with, but there we are. YHA and HI hostels don't, though.

For something a bit homelier, or if you feel the need to have your own space, try Airbnb or Couch Surfing. I had a great experience Couch Surfing with a bunch of girls in their house in Portland, Oregon, a few years ago, and experienced my first (and only) vegan Thanksgiving. I met so many great people in that house, so will always fly the flag for Couch Surfing. As with Airbnb, make sure you read the reviews and feel safe and comfortable with your host. Always do your due diligence and check the testimonials, and if you need extra security, go for verified members only. Also check out BeWelcome and Hospitality Club for a similar service.

One thing I like to do on any trip is take a sleeping bag liner and a pillowcase. For me this is like a little slice of home, and it makes me sleep better. It can also be helpful in less salubrious establishments, shall we say, where cleanliness might not be of the highest order.

If you're happy to hike long distances and carry a tent, then wild camping could be just what you're looking for. It's a fantastic way to switch off and get back to nature. One of my friends, Emily (read her story later in the book), hiked the South West Coastal Path and wild camped along the way. I've hiked solo in Torres del Paine National Park in Chile, and in the Alps of Slovenia, and absolutely love the feeling of being alone in nature and soaking up the fresh air, solitude and peace. It's such a welcome antidote to city living, and there is something extremely soothing and life-affirming about hiking alone. Of course, it's wise to exercise caution – making sure you're fully equipped, that people know where you are, and that you don't veer too far off the marked path, etc. But solo hiking is really a wonderful experience, if done right.

In her book, *Extreme Sleeps*, Phoebe Smith sings the praises of wild camping in off-the-beaten-track locations. And *Wild*, by Cheryl Strayed, about hiking the Pacific Coast Trail, is still one of my all-time favourite stories about solo female travel. Other places to go for inspiration and information include the Ramblers' Association (www.ramblers.org.uk), the brilliant Sian Lewis's blog (thegirloutdoors.co.uk), and Pam the Van's blog (pamthevan.com).

If you don't have much time, and you want to treat

yourself, then why not take yourself off to a fancy hotel for a night (or two)? A friend of mine who has young children makes a regular habit of this, and swears by it to keep her sanity in tact. You don't need to go far, it's more about taking yourself away for some well-deserved self-care than seeing the sights.

Good websites for short-term accommodation

1. Hostelbookers
2. Hostel World
3. Roomer Travel (for discounted hotel rooms)
4. i-escape
5. Mr and Mrs Smith
6. Booking.com (for Europe)
7. Agoda (for Asia)
8. Hotels Combined (for everywhere else)
9. Couchsurfing.com
10. Airbnb

For short-to-medium-term

1. Gumtree (for Europe)
2. Craigslist (for USA)
3. HouseTrip
4. Only Apartments
5. TripAdvisor Rentals
6. FlipKey
7. Homeaway
8. WaytoStay
9. Wimdu

10. Roomarama

11. Lodged Out (unplugged co-living forest camps)

For medium-to-long-term

1. Trusted House Sitters. This website links up people who need someone to mind their house (and sometimes pets) with people who are available to stay in their house for free. Also check out Rover, House Carers, Housesit Match, Mind My House and Nomador. If you're an academic, have a look at Sabbatical Homes. I've done lots of house-sits and pet-sits over the years, and they make a nice change from being on the road all the time, or sharing spaces. As a solo female traveller, they can also be a good way to make friends with locals and feeling part of a community. (And for getting some much-needed peace and quiet.) Though I have to say that sometimes it can be hard work doing everything on your own, and on occasion I have felt a bit unsafe being on my own in a big house. But each house-sit is different, and each person is different, so like everything, it's for you to make up your mind.

2. Home-swaps. If you're lucky enough to be a

home-owner, why not rent your place out, or try a home-swap as a way of seeing the world? You'll have a base from which to explore, and you'll be safe in the knowledge that someone is looking after your pad in return. Good sites to try include Love Home Swap, Home Base Holidays, Stay 4 Free, Home Link and Home Exchange.

3. If you prefer to stay with a local family – and don't want to go through Airbnb due to their sometimes costly add-ons – have a look at Home Stay Finder (homestayfinder.com) and Homestay (www.homestay.com), which lists accommodation in 140 countries. Also check out Worldwide Homestay, Homestay Finder and Bedycasa. If you're travelling in Cuba (which I really recommend), then my personal tip is to stay in *casas particulares* – local homes run by Cuban ladies (very similar to B&Bs in the UK). They can be booked directly over the phone or sometimes via the small tourism booths in the street. Or simply ask your current host to book the next place you're going – they always have friends in other towns and will often phone ahead for you. Cuba is an absolute must for anyone who loves adventure – and will provide a real injection of *joie de vivre*. I had a brilliant time backpacking

around there, dancing salsa in the local clubs, riding horses with cowboys, and drinking mojitos till the cows came home. I did, however, end up in hospital in Havana, but that's a story for another day.

4. Farm Stays. If you've got green fingers and like the idea of staying on a farm or in a rural location, have a look at WWOOF (www.wwoof.net), which links up farm owners with potential volunteers. Farm Stay UK and Farm Stay US are also good.

5. Get a van. Van life has become increasingly popular of late, largely thanks to the rise of Instagram and YouTubers such as Jennelle Eliana, Pam the Van, The Littlest Campervan, A Girl and Her Van, and Tiny Van Big Living. Vans are a great way to combine the freedom of having your own vehicle, with a ready-made place to sleep. I know many girls who've made a great go of van life, especially if they can also work remotely to fund their lifestyles. It's hugely inspiring to watch, even if you don't actually go through with the full van experience yourself. You could always rent one then see if you like it. Portugal is the ideal place to try it out.

Chapter Fifteen

Affording to travel

"It's not enough to be nice in life.
You've got to have nerve."
– Georgia O'Keeffe, American artist

As well as finding the time to travel, finding the money can be equally daunting. Saving up to last a few days, weeks or even months can take longer than expected, but it is possible. If you want something bad enough, there is *always* a way. Mostly it's just a case of working out your priorities in life, and making a few sacrifices. Some people spend their money on physical possessions, others on experiences. Plus, let's not forget that you don't have to fly to the other side of the world to experience the joys that travelling can bring. You can hang out closer to home, go hiking, camping or hostelling in the next town, and have just as fabulous a time. You could try Couchsurfing, house-sitting or Wwoofing in your home country. Travel really doesn't need to break the bank – it's a fallacy that it's an expensive thing to do. What some people spend on a two-week holiday, I could go backpacking on for six months.

If you can, work an extra job, get extra shifts or find a side hustle. Flog your unwanted belongings on eBay. This is a good time to have a clear-out. Squirrel away any extra money for your trip. Put your things in storage or (if you have kind friends and family) in their loft. Minimise your outgoings. You can also plan to work whilst on the road. That way you can stay away for longer, as well as gain valuable skills and lifelong friends. Who knows, you may never come home!

The other thing I'd like to point out is that, depending on where you're from, being away can sometimes be *cheaper* than staying at home. You could become a 'location independent' digital nomad, rent a place in a cheaper country, and work remotely. I once worked out how much it *cost* me to live and work in London, and it was more than if I'd packed a bag and bought a plane ticket out of there. So that's what I did. Sometimes it pays to leave.

Of course, not everyone lives in an expensive city in an expensive country, but you can still run the numbers and ask yourself if you'd be better off where you are, or if it would be cheaper (and you'd be happier) elsewhere. Only you know the answer.

One of my favourite bloggers, Aileen

(www.IamAileen.com), who set up as a freelancer online, recently made a video about how she afforded to travel to all seven continents after leaving her corporate job in the Philippines (which paid her $200 a month). If that doesn't inspire you to get going, nothing will.

It is a huge privilege to be able to travel and see the world, most definitely. To have the time, the money and the health. Let's not forget that. But there are ways and means to squeeze and maximise those things to make it possible. Where there's a will, there's a way, as they say.

Chapter Sixteen

Working on the road

"If it doesn't challenge you, it won't change you."
−Bette Davis, actress.

Here are some ideas for getting work whilst travelling.

1. Freelancing and remote work

If you have a job that can be done on a phone or computer, chances are it can also be done on a beach in Bali. This might sound like a mad idea to those labouring under the iron rod of the nine-to-five, but nothing is stopping you from requesting to work remotely at least some of the time. Your boss can only say no. Start by requesting to work from home one day a week and show them that you are just as productive, if not more so (no commuting, no work chitchat, no pointless meetings, no annoying interruptions from Derek in Accounts). Then build from there.

You could ask to take a sabbatical. Plenty of people have negotiated this and more, so it's just a case of asking and seeing what they say. The reality is that most people will be working remotely or on a freelance basis in the near future, so companies are going to have to get on board with it sooner or later. Quite frankly, I'm amazed that anyone still goes into an office.

The benefit of freelancing is that you get to choose your clients, hours, availability and rate, and work for anyone, from anywhere. For example, freelance copywriters, graphic designers, web developers, virtual assistants, English teachers, tutors, coaches, admins, illustrators, editors, translators, programmers and all manner of other folk can usually work from anywhere on their laptops. You could also consider becoming a consultant.

There are plenty of websites out there to help you find work. The pay isn't always the best, but they can be a good place to start. Have a look at: PeoplePerHour.com, Upwork.com, Freelancer.co.uk, iWriter.com, Guru.com, Fiverr.com, 99designs.com (for graphic designers), tutor.com (for teaching).

2. Teaching English

Teaching English as a foreign language (TEFL) is a great way to live and work abroad. Although it means staying in one place for a period of time, you can always travel at the weekends and school holidays. Teaching can be a great way to integrate and absorb another culture and language before jetting off again, and it's very rewarding. I use to teach English in Paris, and it was one of the most challenging yet rewarding periods of my life.

Many countries are crying out for English teachers, especially in the Middle East and Asia, and will pay you handsomely for your efforts. You'll usually need to be a native English speaker and have a degree and qualification, such as the Trinity TESOL or Cambridge CELTA, but some schools offer short crash courses.

Personally, I recommend paying the extra and getting a bona fide TEFL certificate because it's a great asset to your CV, and you'll be future-proofing your life by being able to work wherever you want in the world. And that is priceless. Check out The Guardian's job page, www.TEFL.com, and Dave's ESL Cafe for job listings.

3. Working with children

A great way to work and save money as a solo female traveller is to become a nanny or au pair. Some families even pay you as well as feed and house you. Have a look at Au Pair World, Great Au Pair, Au Pair, Transitions Abroad, Gumtree, Craigslist, IAPA and Europa Pages.

4. **Ski season**

You could look at doing a ski or snowboard season. Resorts are always looking for experienced instructors. Or if your skills aren't up to scratch you could work as a housekeeper or bartender. If you have your PADI, you could look at diving instructor jobs. Check out Back Door Jobs, About Jobs, Gap Year and Cool Works for overseas job inspiration.

5. **Cruise Ships and Superyachts**

If you've ever dreamed of sailing around the world, then why not sign up to be crew? Some listings don't require you to have any experience, and it could be the adventure of a lifetime.

Working on a cruise ship or superyacht has two main advantages: you get to travel while you work (quite literally), and your salary is tax-free, with hardly any expenses. I know a few people who have worked on superyachts and made a career of it.

Crews on superyachts are a tightly knit bunch, so once you've completed one stint, you'll have a network to reach out to for your second job. Boats always need crew, and if you're ready to travel at the last minute, chances are you'll always find work.

The work on cruise ships is a little different, and much more varied. You can be a croupier, a bartender, a massage therapist, a chef, an entertainer, a yoga teacher, a pot wash, you name it. Cruise ships are like hotels at sea, so whatever you can do in a hotel, you can do on a cruise ship.

The challenge with both jobs is that, whilst at sea, you'll be expected to graft really hard, and be willing to put in the hours with very little time off. But once you're done, you should have earned enough to travel and live well for a good few months.The best way to find work is to head to a boaty location and do the 'dock walk' (handing out your CV to prospects). Alternatively, here are some sites to look for work online: CruiseShipJob.com, Yacht Crew Register, AllCruiseJobs.com, Dock Walk, Find A Crew, Sailing Point, All Cruise Jobs, Cruiser's Forum.

6. **Volunteering**

The website WWOOF (Willing Workers on Organic Farms) lists volunteer placements around the world. The idea is, you trade your time for free bed and board. Hosts usually expect you to work around four hours a day, and this can be in the garden, around the house, or something completely different. It can be a great way to extend your travels, meet some interesting folk, and see a place in a very unique way.

Word of warning: it's great to learn new skills but be mindful of depriving a local person of earning a living. I'll leave it up to you to discern whether or not your work is helping or hindering the local community. And I am just as guilty of this as the next person – there have been a couple of projects (usually in developing countries) that I regret being involved in because they possibly caused more harm than good. The kinds of projects I'm thinking of entail caring for children, any building work, cleaning work, and even reception work in a hostel. I think volunteering can be really positive if approached correctly. But always ask yourself if the job would be better undertaken by a skilled local who could use the money.

Other sites to try for volunteering are: HelpX, Staydu, Anywork Anywhere, International Service (IS), VSO, Peace Corps, Volunteers Base, Grassroots Volunteering, Hostel Jobs, Hostel Travel Jobs, Workaway and Worldpackers.com.

Chapter Seventeen

What to pack

"When preparing to travel, lay out all your clothes and all your money. Then take half the clothes and twice the money." – Susan Heller

Personally I'm a fan of packing as light as possible. One way to do that is to pack your bag, then take everything out, halve it, and re-pack it again. It's amazing how little you need when you're on the road. Most things you think you need, you don't (five pairs of shoes, anyone?). And everything else can usually be bought along the way.

Ideally you should be able to fit everything into a small rucksack and take it on as hand luggage, though I realise this is not always possible. But travelling with a day pack (or small rucksack) means you can be as flexible and nimble as you like, and you're not weighed down with a heap of stuff. Personally, I can't stand wheelie suitcases, especially the larger ones. They play havoc with your back, trip up those people behind you, and make tackling stairs, hills and public transport a nightmare. I can't understand why anyone would use one. I like to take a small, soft bag that can be squeezed into all kinds of spaces. A day pack is ideal because you can distribute the weight across your shoulders, often tying it around your waist so you hardly feel it. But a soft holdall is also good.

I take a small rucksack for trips lasting up to a month, then take my larger backpack for any camping trips or longer, more complex travels. Being able to run for a bus or train when everyone else is lugging their massive Samsonites around is extremely liberating. And you never have to plan what you're doing more than a few hours in advance because you're not carrying anything that prevents you from going with the flow. This mindset is ideal for the solo traveller, who often wants to change plans at the last minute and get from A to B quickly and cheaply.

I also like to start packing as far in advance as possible. I build up a pile of things in the corner of the room, and add to it as new items occur to me. Then it's just a case of assembling it all together 1-2 days before. I also keep a list in my journal for each trip I do, and write down anything I wish I'd brought with me, or that I had to buy, so that next time I come back to the same place, I'll be more prepared. Then I take a picture of the contents of my rucksack so I can recreate it easily.

This is an example of a bare-bones packing list:

Passport

Credit cards

The clothes you're wearing

An extra change of clothes

Spare underwear

A toothbrush

A towel

Essential medication.

Things to pack in your hand luggage:

1. A packet of tissues.

2. A small bottle of anti-bacterial hand sanitiser.

3. A travel toothbrush and small toothpaste.

4. Earplugs. My personal favourites are Muffles from Boots in the UK.

5. A pair of headphones. I like my noise-cancelling headphones, but some people find them too bulky and uncomfortable and prefer ear buds instead.

6. A camera, smartphone, tablet and/or laptop.

All electronics should be kept in your hand luggage rather than your checked bag, which makes them susceptible to damage and theft whilst in transit.

7. A clean pair of underwear, in case your luggage gets lost or is delayed.

8. A scarf for keeping warm on air-conditioned transport, as well as for use as a pillow. (A friend of mine swears by her Therm-a-Rest pillow for travelling.)

9. Any essential medication.

10. Moisturiser and lip balm.

11. A hat and sunglasses.

In your main backpack or suitcase

Use plastic bags or mesh laundry bags to separate out similar-themed items and make them much easier to find. Using plastic bags is a little noisy (we've all been woken by the bag-rustler in hostel dorms, and they're never the most popular of people). But the upside is they keep your belongings dry should your bag get wet. Mesh bags are see-through, saving you time.

1. One lightweight, smart outfit – dress, or shirt and trousers – that will do you for a fancy dinner or meeting.

2. One pair of smart shoes or sandals.

3. One travel towel plus a sarong. The towel does the drying, the sarong does the covering up, both on the beach and in the bathroom (I always keep them separate, and never take my travel towel to the beach). In hot countries, you can soak your sarong overnight to wash it then wear it as a cape to keep you cool and covered. If you're given towels at your accommodation, and you don't have air conditioning, you can wet the towels and use them as a pillow and blanket. They will stay cool throughout the night and allow you to sleep.

4. Two cotton tops or T-shirts, preferably with sleeves to avoid offending anyone or getting sunburned.

5. One pair of lightweight trousers for day wear.

6. One pair of sturdy shoes for day wear. These can be hiking shoes or trainers but they need to double for city walking and country walking, as you might be doing a bit of both. These are the shoes you'll wear the most, and the ones you'll fly in, so invest in a good pair.

7. Take more underwear than you think you'll need. I usually take 14 days' worth on a long trip. For all other items, I pack for one week, then just wash as I go.

8. Safety pins and a roll of gaffer tape for reinforcing cables, taping up mosquito net holes, taping over any glaring brand names on expensive items, holding your bag together if it falls apart, your clothes together if they fall apart, you if you fall apart, fixing curtains to walls for extra privacy, and creating makeshift purses and pockets underneath your clothes and bed.

9. A pair of rubber gloves, a nail brush and a few clothes pegs for hand-washing on the go. You can use your solid shampoo bar or a special detergent bar to wash with (I've found these in South Africa and India but you can also buy them online). The best way to wash your clothes is to fill a sink, bucket or bath with hot water, add in your clothes and your bar of soap, then leave them to soak for at least an hour. I then don my rubber gloves, and, under a running tap, scrub any soiled areas. I then refill the sink with cold water and rinse the clothes. Once all the soap is gone, I twist them to get rid of as much water as possible before placing

each item one at a time onto a dry towel, rolling it up, and twisting again inside the towel (I fix one end with my knees and twist the other with my hands). When you release the towel, the garment can then be hung up – ideally on hangers – to dry. If you have a fan in your room, place it near the clothes, and they dry very quickly this way. Then do a proper laundry session every week or so.

10. A travel hairdryer for drying your hair, blasting damp clothes and heating up your bed before you get in. An absolute lifesaver.

11. A hot water bottle for stomach cramps, period pains, back pain and keeping you warm in cold countries.

12. An umbrella for rain and sun. You can walk around all day in a hot country and not get sunstroke or sunburn.

13. A hand fan. Any cheap fan will do, but if you're going anywhere in Asia you can pick up some lovely foldable ones in the markets. Buy a couple, just in case you lose one. Use in conjunction with the umbrella and a cold towel for walking around hot countries. I soak a flannel in cold water before I go out – that way it stays damp and cool the

whole day and is nice to dab on the face and neck.

14. A travel kettle. You may think this is overkill, but I never go anywhere without my little kettle because it makes endless cups of tea and coffee, which saves me a fortune, and also boils my water to make it drinkable, thus saving on copious amounts of plastic.

15. A thermos bottle. Take two if you can fit them in. These will keep your water ice cold. I like to store mine overnight in a freezer compartment, if there is one, then carry it in my handbag during the day, which keeps me nice and cool. Similarly, boil up some water and make a hot thermos for cold days. In many countries, the water isn't drinkable. And this means hell for the environment. In Thailand you can fill water bottles on the street for a few cents. If you're going to be anywhere for long, stock up on big bottles of water and decant them each day. Or boil your own and use your thermos to cool them down in.

TOP TIP:

"Some of the things I always like to take with me are Marmite, Earl Grey tea, and a tiny coffee maker. Slightly more practically, cable ties, super glue and gorilla tape – a combination that can fix practically anything. Also, a small rubber door wedge can give peace of mind in bedrooms/bathrooms without proper locks on the door." Emily Chrystie, 29, from Devon, UK

In your toiletries bag:

1. Solid shampoo bar (cut this in half just in case you leave one half in a bathroom somewhere. Keep one half in your hand luggage, in case your main bag is lost or delayed, and the other in your checked bag). This will be fine for washing hair, skin and clothes. One bar can last 1-2 months. If you can, get one with tea tree oil as this will help ward off any bugs and mosquitos.

2. Crystal, solid or powder deodorant. Again, this lasts months and will save on space.

3. A spare credit card sequestered inside a pocket of a toiletries or make-up bag.

4. Essential oils (these can be roll-on or spray). I swear by tea tree (for bites, spots, mosquitos), peppermint (for headaches and stomach ache), lavender (for sleep and burns – including sunburn), coconut (for dry skin), and oregano (anti-viral – use very sparingly).

5. Baking powder toothpaste. Tastes gross but lasts for ages and never leaks.

6. Clear SPF50 sun spray. I personally love sun sprays as they're lightweight and you can reach the middle of your back and other awkward areas, without having to enlist the help of a stranger (awkward).

7. A tube of industrial-strength moisturiser, such as E45 cream, Nivea cream or Savlon for inevitable dry skin syndrome.

8. A strong hair clip to keep curtains closed and mosquito nets in place. And possibly to actually stick your hair up.

Chapter Eighteen

Staying healthy while travelling

"The world is a book, and those who do not travel read only a page." Saint Augustine

Always book an appointment with your doctor as soon as you've bought your flight, so you can discuss any vaccinations or medication you might need. The sooner you do this, the better, as sometimes they have to order in the correct items.

It can be really difficult to stay healthy when travelling. Not only do you have the obvious challenges of tummy bugs, insects, foreign bacteria, food and water to contend with, you can often let your exercise routine slip, or fall into an unhealthy eating habit. It's good to enjoy yourself, and let go of the rigid chains of 21st-century living, and it's not always practical to live up to the same ideals you hold for yourself at home. I used to come home from long trips at least a stone heavier, and completely out of shape. Nowadays, I'm much better at looking after myself. Aside from any medication, there are a few items that I always pack with me, to try and stay as healthy as I can. Here are a few of them:

1. Avoid insect bites as much as possible. Cover up your skin with your sarong or scarf, and wear long, loose-fitting clothing. There are plenty of natural alternatives to DEET, which is so strong it once melted my passport. You can add tea tree oil to your shower gel and sun cream to help repel insects. Pack a couple of small clickers for bites. They're a revelation. And keep a repellent tea tree oil in your handbag and dab it around your wrists and ankles – especially around 4pm when they like to come out to play. My preferred shop-bought repellent is called Peaceful Sleep from South Africa, which smells lovely.

2. Acidophilus. Take it every day and drink at least three litres of water, one before breakfast.

3. Carry some tubes of soluble, high-dose vitamin C and zinc tablets, and add one or two of these to your bottle of drinking water each day.

3. I also carry plenty of rehydration sachets, and add one to my drinking water each day.

4. Pack a good supply of multivitamins to ensure you get all the nutrients you need.

5. Carry enough of your contraceptive pill, if you take one. You don't want to run out of this. Same with condoms.

6. Pack a menstrual cup. Not only are these safer and more convenient than tampons, they're much better for the environment as not all countries dispose of sanitary waste properly. You can leave a menstrual cup in for longer than you would a tampon, so there's less pressure to be in a place where you can change it regularly. Take a bottle of water into the bathroom and use this to rinse it out. I also carry tissues in my handbag, just in case the toilet doesn't have enough paper.

7. Walk as much as you can during the day, if it's safe to do so. This is a great way to see the sights, stay fit and healthy, and get plenty of vitamin D. Always wear sunscreen and a hat, plus comfortable shoes, and don't forget to carry your umbrella, plus plenty of water and a map on your phone (like Maps.me). If you're a runner, this is also a great way to discover new places, though again, be careful not to get lost or run into trouble.

8. It can be difficult to do yoga or any stretching whilst sleeping in a dorm, but it is possible. Use your bunk to do some basic stretching. You can also do yoga in the shower, the toilet cubicle or at the beach. Check out Yoga With Adriene on YouTube for ideas. Or join a local class!

9. Gym bunnies can research local gyms or swimming pools. Or hit the beach and exercise there.

10. The sun can be your worst enemy, even though that might be why you went travelling in the first place. I've seen more than my fair share of burned skin, and now cannot think of anything worse. Lather on SPF50 first thing in the morning to give it time to sink in before you get dressed, then carry your spray around in your bag to top up during the day. Wear a hat, and cover up as best you can. I promise you, skin cancer ain't fun. Nor is sun burn, sun stroke, tan lines or wrinkles. Pack a bottle of aloe vera gel for any accidental situations.

11. Take a good supply of Alka-Seltzer soluble sachets, a jar of tiger balm for headaches and period pains, milk thistle tablets for any overindulgent nights, a course of antibiotics for

emergencies, and a bottle of Flying Rabbit stomach settler from Thailand (or Pepto-Bismol equivalent).

12. Lately, I've also started packing herbal tinctures, such as wormwood – for parasites, viruses and worms – and valerian to help me sleep.

13. Gynopedia is a free online resource for female sexual health information around the world. You simply search by city, and Gynopedia gives you the local lowdown on birth control, abortion clinics and STI testing. https://gynopedia.org

Chapter Nineteen

Staying safe

———————

"Security is mostly a superstition. It does not exist in nature, nor do the children of men as a whole experience it. Avoiding danger is no safer in the long run than outright exposure. Life is either a daring adventure, or nothing." – Helen Keller, American author, activist and lecturer

Ah, safety - the age-old question! It's the biggest concern for anyone thinking of setting off alone. And there is no simple answer. I mean, it's not like there are completely safe places and completely dangerous places, since bad things can happen anywhere, at any time. Many of the things that can happen in another country can happen in your home country. I often read of truly tragic stories in my home town.

Statistically, though, certain countries have higher crime rates than others. However, the figures are mostly focused on local residents. For example, according to the Foreign Office, 154,586 British nationals visited Brazil in 2018, and despite high crime levels in the country, most visits were trouble-free. Plus, girls and women tend to experience different kinds of crimes.

It's a similar story with South Africa. "Isn't it dangerous?" is the one question I get asked whenever I talk about it. And I never know how to answer it. Because, in many other ways, South Africa feels a hundred times friendlier and more positive than at home. I love the upbeat vibrancy of the place, the lifestyle, the landscapes, music, food and culture. I've been extremely lucky to have made friends with amazing poets, musicians, artists, entrepreneurs, activists and film-makers, and had some incredible experiences that's I'll remember for the rest of my life. Yet if you look at the crime statistics, you'd never set foot in the place.

The official line from the Foreign Office is: "Most violent crimes tend to occur in townships, isolated areas and away from the normal tourist destinations. Over 430,000 British tourists visit South Africa each year. Most visits are trouble-free, but a small number of British people encounter problems in South Africa."

That said, it's the one place I've experienced a mugging in broad daylight, plus I've had my backpack slashed open and belongings stolen in a hostel dorm, so you do have to have your wits about you. I would never walk the streets at night there. In fact, I'd be mindful of walking in many places alone – day or night. Thankfully, Ubers are very cheap and common there, plus you have the Baz Bus, which will take you from hostel to hostel.. So I think it's a great place to travel around – you just have to adjust your behaviour accordingly, and abide by its rules. And every place has its rules.

Some of my worst experiences, shall we say, have been in the UK and Europe. As you'll read later in this book, my friend Rachel absolutely adored being alone in Italy. Yet my sister and I backpacked around there in our early-twenties and had a terrible time of it. We were despised by the women, and constantly harassed by the men. Which just goes to show that one woman's hell is another's heaven.

Japan is mostly wonderful, but I've heard of girls being followed in smaller towns. And don't even think of showing off your tattoos (or shoulders, for that matter). Portugal is generally very safe but, as we know, bad things can happen anywhere. I had a terrible experience there once, in a park in Porto, and nobody came to my aid, plus the police didn't even want to hear about it. I still go back to Portugal all the time, because I love it and because I refuse to let one bad experience keep me down.

Certainly, my feelings – and experiences – surrounding the issue of safety have changed a lot over the years. I'm definitely not as gung-ho as I used to be, and there are many situations I wouldn't put myself in now, that 10-20 years ago I wouldn't have thought twice about. I'm not sure if this is down to age, or whether the world feels like a more hostile, judgemental place now. Perhaps a bit of both. It's assumed that as we get older we become more confident – but perhaps we become more cautious, and wiser, too.

I've also noticed there are new things to watch out for. Not so long ago it was rare for people to own long-lens SLR cameras and smartphones. Now they're commonplace. So it's easier for women to be photographed, videoed and shared wherever, without their knowledge or consent. I've noticed much surreptitious picture-taking on beaches, poolsides and in parks and cafes. It can leave you feeling robbed and violated, especially if you're minding your own business trying to relax. But there's very little you can do about it, bar chasing someone down the street and wrestling their phone off them.

It's why I feel the issue of safety and danger is very nuanced and complicated. Two different people can have two different experiences in the same place. Personally, I hardly ever talk about safety with men (or couples), because they usually give terrible advice and have no idea what my concerns and criteria for safety even are.

When a man or a couple or a group might decide to do something spontaneously, the solo female traveller will have to weigh it up carefully, and possibly think twice about doing it at all. That's not to say she can't or won't do it – it's just she'll have to look at it from all angles, roll it around in her mind, and plan accordingly.

Do you go for that hike on your own? Do you camp overnight or find a hotel? Do you walk back along the beach or take the main road? Or call a taxi or rickshaw that may be driven by a dodgy man? What's less risky? Do you check out of that guesthouse where the manager always chats you up? Where is the exit? Do you continue down that road or turn back? Do you take that shortcut or go the long way round? Do you go to the market or wait for someone to join you? Where can I go to the toilet? A woman will filter potentially hundreds of these situations each and every day.

So, as a solo traveller, although you don't have to compromise with a partner, friend or group, you still have to compromise with your environment. A lot. You might not be able to do everything you want to do, or go everywhere you want to go. This can be a hard pill to swallow for anyone who's used to being treated on a par with the guys, or who's grown up with anonymity, independence, respect and unbridled freedom.

One thing I will say is that, although there will probably be hassle and annoyances, rarely will a situation become an emergency (though, of course, emergencies can happen). I call this "the middle band" of danger, because in most places, rarely will you be 100% safe and rarely will you be 100% in danger – most of the time you'll be somewhere in the middle. Women have to deal with many "micro-violations" and "micro-aggressions", and these can be subtle, non-verbal and/or non-physical, and therefore very difficult to quantify and articulate. Feeling limited in what you can do, intimidated, patronised or stared at are a few such examples. Dealing with this middle band can take up a lot of energy and mental bandwidth, and, if you're alone a lot, can get quite tiring.

Women often don't report these incidents – either because they feel the situation is too minor, or they're too embarrassed or traumatised to recount the ordeal, or they fear it will get them in trouble. So statistics aren't all that reliable. There's also the chance they won't be believed or taken seriously. You only need to look at the newspapers today to see how women who report incidents of harassment and assault are treated and talked about.

You'll have a constant thrum of awareness running through you, like a computer program running in the background. Even when a girl looks like she's relaxed and having fun, a primal part of her brain, whether she's aware of it or not, will be on high alert keeping her safe. I believe this isn't so different whether you're at home or abroad.

In the first instance, it is ALWAYS better to be safe than sorry. Your safety should be your number one priority. Your best ally will be your body and intuition. Listen to them. You could take a self-defence course to feel more empowered physically (I recommend Krav Maga or Wing Chun), but developing and listening to your intuition will be your first port of call. Build that muscle, trust it and don't be afraid to follow what it says, even if you feel silly doing so. Maybe everything seems fine on the outside, but your gut says, "Hmm, this feels a bit off". It's your gut you want to listen to. Walk away and save yourself any regrets.

It seems obvious to say this, but so many people flout their personal safety on a daily basis. Don't take unnecessary risks or put yourself in dangerous situations. Use your common sense. Ask yourself, "Would I feel OK if my sister, niece, mother or daughter were doing this?" If not, don't. Just don't. It's better to err on the side of caution than regret it.

Every country and city has its own particular brand of annoyances and threats. For example, in Ethiopia I was followed incessantly, and had, not one, but two stalkers, which was unnerving to say the least.

In India, if I stood still for more than three seconds, a group of men would gather round me and start taking pictures of me on their phones. Not in an inquisitive way, but in a really creepy, up-to-no-good kind of way. (Side note: I was covered up and dressed extremely conservatively the whole time.)

Now, a guy isn't going to understand how this feels because he's rarely, if ever, been subjected to it. It's a foreign language to him. A man would tell you to just shrug this kind of thing off. No harm done. What's the problem? Because there is no accurate equivalent for guys. But I would file all this kind of behaviour under the middle-band of threats – the annoyances and micro-violations that are hard to quantify or report.

Some people still assume females bring this sort of thing upon themselves by the way they dress, behave, speak, breathe, live, think, eat, drink, anything (it MUST be our fault). By the way, if you ever do travel around India on your own, I recommend renting a motorbike or scooter. Bye-bye staring men! (Though they did still throw rocks at me.)

I'm not saying all of this to put you off or scare you. Quite the opposite. I think it's important to go into solo travel prepared, with eyes wide open.

It's a case of weighing up the pros and cons, doing your research, and making wise decisions. I'm all for getting out of the comfort zone, but also preparing as best you can for what might greet you at the other end.

Preparation is key. If you can, listen and talk to other women who've been there. Read up on the local cultures and customs so when you land you are fully briefed and less likely to make a faux pas or put yourself in danger due to ignorance. Being forewarned is forearmed.

Check your official security departments – ideally before booking your ticket. In the UK, it's the Foreign Office: fco.gov.uk. In the US, it's travel.state.gov, in Canada it's voyage.gc.ca, and in Australia it's dfat.gov.au. These sites will give you up-to-date information on the locations you're thinking of travelling to, and I recommend cross-referencing these with each other, as well as with recent guidebooks and forums, because many problems are very time-sensitive and localised and might not affect you.

I also want to say that sometimes travelling on your own can be safer than travelling with a partner, friend, or as part of a group – as strange as that may seem. My spidey senses are finely tuned when I'm alone, but when I'm with others, I tend to let go more, and my intuition gets crowded out. And if my travel partner is a bit free-wheeling, well then we can get into all kinds of scrapes. In fact, some of my most nail-biting moments have been whilst travelling with others (male and female). If I'd been alone, it's likely none of these things would have happened.

Chapter Twenty

Some safety tips

---

1. It's an obvious one, but try to dress and behave in a way that's culturally appropriate to your environment, and by that I mean err on the side of caution, even in Western countries. I find that dressing up or down, as the situation requires, helps me blend in. Keep jewellery to a minimum, if worn at all. Personally I find it uncomfortable and one more thing to think about, plus it sometimes attracts attention. Some women swear by wearing a wedding ring to deter any potential admirers. Another idea is to dye your hair. I also like to carry a sarong or scarf, and wrap it around my whole body. A sarong is like an invisibility cape – it conceals all manner of things.

2. Avoid confrontation as best you can.

3. Avoid large crowds and demonstrations.

4. Don't get too close to wildlife, and certainly don't try and touch it. Unless you're in a petting zoo or a cat cafe.

5. Body language speaks volumes. A confident

person is less likely to be marked out as a victim. Don't worry if you don't "feel confident" right away. It will get easier and easier with each day.

6. The way you walk will inform how others behave around you. I've experimented with walking really fast, and walking slowly. Both work well in different situations. Sometimes walking fast makes you stand out more or look scared, and walking slowly (not dawdling) means you can pass by unnoticed, especially if you're quiet. Other times, walking fast means that nobody bothers you because you have a purposeful air about you and – more accurately – it's hard to keep up with you, and most people are lazy. Both fast and slow have their uses.

7. In bars, it's a good idea to buy your own drinks and keep them within sight at all times – and to keep a hand over your glass or bottle while you're talking.

8. Maintain your boundaries and your "fence". If someone gets too close, subtly move away. Different cultures have very different ideas of what constitutes personal space, so it doesn't necessarily mean what you think it means. Usually asking that person politely to move away is enough for them to back it up a little.

9. Using humour can often get you out of a sticky situation and defuse a potential threat.

10. If it's not overtly dangerous, but you feel someone is acting strange, you can also try acting little bit strange, too – they're rarely expecting this. Start laughing really loudly at nothing, or shouting at nobody, it can often put a wannabe hassler/attacker off.

11. Another trick I use quite a lot if I feel under moderate threat (not extreme), is to pretend I'm pregnant. Let's say you're walking down the street and feel a bit unsafe, or you're on a bus and get a bad vibe from someone, but can't, for whatever reason, move, or you feel that making a scene would make it worse. These are times where I pretend to be pregnant. You might think it would be hard to do, but look at how a pregnant woman walks and holds herself – it's very easy to replicate, even if you don't have an obvious bump. I rub my lower belly, my lower back, put my hands out to feel the seat before I sit down, and walk slowly with a kind of arched back. In most countries, people are extremely respectful of pregnant women. Of course, if anyone is intent on causing you harm, they'll do so whether you're with child or not. But most of the time, you won't

be dealing with extremists, and acting pregnant can get you out of many scrapes.

12. I also use the fake phone call. If I'm in a taxi or restaurant or any place where I feel I may potentially be a target (though don't whip your phone out anywhere it may be stolen), I pretend I'm calling my boyfriend or husband. I have a "conversation" with this person, and relay the details of where I am, who I'm with and what time I'll be back. If I'm in a taxi, I say something like: "I'm on my way to you now, I should only be about 5-10 minutes, see you soon." Sometimes I'll even go so far as to say, "I'll text you the registration plate." Then I set an alarm on my phone to ring in five minutes' time. When the alarm goes off, I pretend that it's the boyfriend/husband calling me back to check up on me. I reassure him once again that I'll be there very soon, say a few more words, then end the call. I nearly always see the taxi driver look in their rear-view mirror while I'm talking. I also send a message to a friend to let them know where I am, and (if I'm using Uber or Lyft) share my journey with someone who's in the same town, or any friend who is online so they know my whereabouts.

13. You can deploy the element of surprise and then

use that split second while they're thinking to run away. For example, someone approaches you and asks for money or tries harassing you or whatever, you can say something like, "I think I know your mother" or "Do you want that in dollars or Euros?" or anything else that might confuse them for a second. Then run.

14. Leave details of your travel itinerary with a reliable person at home, as well as with a trustworthy contact in the country you're visiting. Have your local contact's number saved in your phone. Also save your hotel or hostel's number. And two local taxi numbers.

15. Keep valuables, credit cards, cameras and passports out of sight – ideally locked in a safe at your hotel or hostel. Otherwise wrapped around you close to your skin.

16. Keep all the car doors locked whenever you're inside the vehicle. Park your car in well-lit areas, preferably those that have guards on duty. Lock your belongings in the boot, or, ideally never keep any valuables inside. If driving in more dangerous countries – especially in Africa – consider fitting anti-shatter film to all windows in the car.

17. Take a whistle or personal alarm with you everywhere you go. Not only is this useful if you're

attacked, it will help you be found should you get lost or, God forbid, caught in a fire or earthquake.

18. I like to keep my small purse down my bra. This contains the basics I need for the day – minimum cash, one bank card, plus room key and padlock key. I've never lost this purse, ever. I usually also carry a decoy purse in a bag that I wear across my body. This is the purse that has non-essentials, and enough cash to make it believable in case you have to hand it over. I also keep a credit card in a secret location in my main backpack wherever I'm staying, and spare cash and bank cards locked in a safe. That way, I'm never left high and dry financially. Yes, it takes a bit of getting used to having a purse down your bra, as well as needing to reach down your top to pay for stuff, but I've never had any problems with it, and most people seem to understand exactly what I'm doing and why. Plus, if you're wearing a scarf as a shawl (or cape), it hides everything. The added bonus is that, if anyone goes to grope you, they'll have a nasty surprise.

19. Don't feel pressured to be nice. It's engrained in girls from a young age to be nice, but if someone's hassling you, don't be afraid of cutting them off. That said, I sometimes find that ignoring someone

or smiling and gently and saying no thanks, then turning away, is enough to get them to leave me alone, and that if I'd shouted at them or been rude, it would have escalated the situation unnecessarily. I've also used the "ice maiden" technique a lot, whereby I've completely blanked whoever I can feel is up to no good, and fixed a "don't mess with me" look on my face whilst gazing into the middle distance. I also deploy humour as necessary. People aren't always expecting that. But do what feels right for you in the moment. If someone crosses your boundaries, don't be afraid to tell them so.

20. If you suspect someone is following you, simply cross the road and casually notice what they do. If they cross as well, then slow down rather than speed up. If they slow down too, try stopping and see what happens. I find most of the time, this person walks on. The point is, you want this person in front of you, not behind. You can also pretend you forgot something, and turn around and walk in the opposite direction. If they still follow, then walk into the nearest bar, shop or cafe, where you can assess the situation and call the police or a taxi if needs be.

21. Be wary of reporting cases of rape in Dubai,

Afghanistan, Saudi Arabia, Somalia, and even Ireland – amazingly, this will often backfire on you or incriminate you. Rather than you being the victim of a heinous crime, you'll likely be thrown in jail for having "illicit sex". We live in a mad, mad world.

22. Try carrying a folder or laptop case around to look official and like you're on business. I often carry my laptop around anyway as it's part of my job, but in places where it would be unsafe to do so, I simply carry the case filled with paperwork and magazines. I hold this close to my chest and I walk with purpose (not necessarily fast – a slow walk can be just as meaningful – see above). This detracts from wannabe hasslers, commands more respect, and – as with the above purse example – acts as a concealer and shield, should anyone go in for a grope. If I'm feeling really scared, then I repeat in my head, "I am a teacher/doctor/lawyer and I'm here to see someone very important." This informs the way I walk. The only time this has backfired on me was in South Africa when I stupidly walked back from a local cafe to my Airbnb carrying my actual laptop. A guy on a bike cycled past me, and must have clocked my laptop, because he then circled around and cycled straight

up the pavement and directly into me, then went to grab my computer. Thankfully I'd taken the self-defence course and, although it all happened very quickly, and I was in shock, I managed to fight him off while swearing at the top of my voice, "Get the F away from me!" (He ended up in the middle of the road, while I ran for my life.) But this is not a good situation. Obviously if someone has a weapon, it's a no-brainer. You hand them the laptop.

23. Pack a bike lock, bike lights and head torch. The lock is used to secure your bag to a solid object on long bus or train journeys, or in your room if there's no safe or locker. The lights and head torch are used when walking after dark, or when reading late and moving around your dorm at night, so as not to wake other people. Both, of course, are also useful for when you hire a bike. Just remember to separate out the keys, and pack them in different compartments, so you always have a spare.

24. In any situation, identify someone who looks safe, and who might be able to help if things go wrong. Women and families are usually a good bet, and anyone in a position of authority. You'll know who to choose by the way they look and

carry themselves. Sit next to them if appropriate or possible. Even better, strike up a conversation with them. In the UK, there is a brilliant new initiative called Ask For Angela, where bar staff are trained to help any woman in a difficult situation. You simply go up to the bar and ask for Angela. It would be great if this was rolled out internationally as it's such a good idea.

25. As best you can, try and sit at the front of the bus, near the driver, and never at the back. Tell the driver where you're going, and don't get off unless you're sure you're exactly where you need to be. If you feel someone near you is behaving strangely or acting inappropriately, simply move and sit next to a woman, if there is one around. Or alert the driver. In some countries there are women-only train carriages. I wish this were the norm everywhere.

26. Report any wrongdoing to an official as soon as possible (though be wary of reporting rape in some countries). They may or may not listen or believe you, but get it down in writing and take a photo of the document and any names of the officials you spoke to.

27. Pack a rubber door stop, and use it to give extra security to your bedroom door, or a bathroom. It's

not foolproof, but will help you in places where you might not trust the locks (or management) 100%.

28. Pack a range of padlocks. I use one large one for my main rucksack, and smaller ones for my hand luggage. They also come in handy to use in lockers and as makeshift safes with your rucksack, if there isn't one in the room, because rarely will someone come in and steal your whole bag. More likely they will take what is lying around. Most theft is of the opportunistic variety. Keep all zips locked as often as you can. Although this isn't failsafe (I've had my backpack slashed open before whilst locked in a dorm room), it will act as a deterrent. Obviously if there is a safe, use it. I'm really strict about this, after I've had a couple of negative experiences – even in five-star hotels. I always lock up my valuables and documents, as well as anything that would be difficult to replace, such as my journal, passport, USB sticks and notebooks.

29. Consider hiring a scooter or bicycle – this can be a good way to see an area and cover a lot of ground. It also helps you avoid touts and hasslers and avoid the arguments with rickshaw drivers. If you do rent a bike, motorbike or scooter, remember to wear a jacket, cardigan or wrap a

sarong around you to keep you warm and protect you from the sun. Pack your own bike lights and personal locks and use them. I also pack my high-vis vest as it's so lightweight. Step off it to the side, don't swing your legs over, and don't forget to kick up the stand. You'd be amazed how easy it is to forget, then ride off with sparks flying as you scrape up the road.

30. Ask a female who works in your hotel or hostel if there are any particular areas or things to avoid. If you ask a man, or a couple, you won't get an accurate answer. Always seek out a woman who's around the same age, if you can, because they'll know what's what.

31. Make sure your smartphone is fully charged before going out, and take a power bank with you in case the battery dies.

32. Be mindful of telling someone that you're alone, or where you're staying. People will ask about these two things all the time, and be wary of how much you tell them.

33. Carry a business card from the hostel or hotel you're staying in. If you get lost you can always ask for directions or hand the card to a taxi driver to take you back there. Similarly, ask the front desk of your accommodation for a couple of local taxi

numbers before you go out. Take a picture of all these business cards on your phone for safekeeping.

34. Wandering around and "getting lost" (if it's safe to do so) is one of the joys of travelling, and can lead to all kinds of adventures, meetings, stories and discoveries. Download a PDF guidebook on your phone, plus an offline map, such as Maps.me. Then I like to mark where I'm staying, and any points of interest in the area (such as food recommendations I've researched beforehand). That way, I always know how to get back, and can riff around the place safely.

35. Consider downloading a personal safety app that links you to friends and family back home. If you're not back by the time you said you would be, or if something awry happens, your designated people are alerted right away. Try Find My Friends and bSafe. Personally, I value my freedom and privacy, that's the whole point of going away, but I can see the value in these apps for keeping loved-ones' minds at rest.

36. Learn some of the local language, or at the very least download a free offline translator app so you can be understood in an emergency.

Chapter Twenty-One

Some self-defence techniques

In my own experience, the things that have kept me out of danger were less to do with physical prowess, and more to do with being smart, savvy and occasionally funny. That said, having a few moves up your sleeve can be no bad thing.

Only on two occasions have I had to resort to physical violence. I took a self-defence course a couple of years ago and honestly wished I'd learned this stuff at school. I wish all girls were taught self-defence at school. Knowing how to protect yourself gives you the confidence to fight back if someone tries to physically harm you.

I've outlined what the teacher taught me, mixed in with some of my own tips I've picked up along the way. It's up to you what you deem appropriate under the circumstances, but if someone attacks you, you can do whatever it takes (using reasonable force) to defend yourself until the threat is over.

1. As best you can, no matter what happens, try not to go to ground. Once you're on the ground, you're

in the weakest position possible. Do everything in your power to remain standing, so you can fight and run.

2. Make as much noise as possible. I mean, REALLY go for it. This can often be enough to ward off a potential attacker. Most attackers want to control you, so if you make a scene, you're more difficult to control – plus others will hopefully hear you and come to your aid. Only use violence as a last resort.

3. If you do decide to fight, then commit to it.

2. Try not to punch. Unless you're trained in martial arts, punching will probably cause you more harm than your assailant. Instead, a good alternative is to use the base of your hand or the side of your hand (known as a "hammer fist"), and target the eyes, nose and throat. The base of a hand against a nose can be very effective.

3. Use your nails, elbows, teeth, a set of keys, a ballpoint pen, anything. A knuckle into the ribs, sternum or throat is very painful. Bite, scratch, pinch and kick, and aim for the weak points. Grab testicles, pinch inside the arms and legs, kick shins and the tops of feet.

4. A good technique to deploy is the "horse tail" – a quick flick of the nails in your assailant's eyes.

This looks more like a backhanded slap than a stabbing motion. But just focus on your nails making contact with their eyes, and you should be fine.

5. Instead of going to kick your attacker in the groin (allowing them to grab your leg and throw you down), kick their shins or stamp on the top of their feet, ideally scraping down the shin as you go.

6. If anyone grabs you from the front, lift your arms up in front of you (as if your wrists are tied together), then quickly move your arms to the side to break their hold. If they do manage to grab you, use your teeth to bite them hard, stamp on their feet with your heels, and use your thumb knuckle to rub in between their finger joints on the top hand until they release you. You can also pinch the insides of their arms, use your elbows into their stomach or groin and use your heels on their shins.

7. If someone grabs your wrist, place your other hand on top of their hand to secure it, then straighten your hand (the one that's being grabbed, keeping fingers together) and circle it in a clockwise motion (clockwise for right hand, anti-clockwise for left) to escape the grab.

8. If they've grabbed both your wrists, quickly whip your hands out and in to bang their thumbs together.

9. You can move someone away from you very effectively by making a V shape with your hand between the thumb and index finger, and pushing it into their throat, simultaneously pushing up and walking them backwards until they fall.

10. If (God forbid) you should find yourself in a rape or sexual assault situation, try and pee yourself there and then. Also tell them you're pregnant. This can be enough to stop the act in its tracks.

11. If your assailant is on top of you, press your thumb knuckle into their sternum, ribs or throat, and if you can, hook your leg under theirs and kick the back of their knee.

Chapter Twenty-Two

Stories from the road

"You and I are more than friends. We're like a really small gang." – Thelma and Louise

I met each of the following ladies while travelling. They all inspired me in different ways with their stories, and I hope they inspire you, too.

Lam Duong, 30, is a doctor and lives in Berlin. We met in a hostel in Seville, Spain.

My boyfriend and I broke up just two weeks before we were due to start our trip to New Zealand. My family, especially my mother, was wondering why I would still want to travel, since the decision to do so was based upon me and my boyfriend having time alone together before settling down. After the break-up I couldn't travel right away because I felt I had to figure out what I wanted to do, where I wanted to go, and what my purpose was in travelling... So I decided to sublet my apartment in Berlin and first move to my hometown in Ulm for two months to spend time with my family and also work with my mum in her restaurant.

Although I knew I should use this opportunity of being free of work, and also financially free, moving back with my family after the break-up was very comforting, and thoughts like, "Hmmm, I am happy like this and it wouldn't be too bad to find a new job and start working again and not do this trip... And isn't it also a very big step doing this trip alone? Won't I feel lonely, etc?" started to pop up in my head. Staying at home felt comforting and more secure.

I'm lucky that I have a handful of friends who are free spirits, and when talking to them I knew that I had to use this chance to travel. So I started to make plans: What did I want get out of this trip? Are there skills I want to gain? Is there a language I have always wanted to learn? What is my profession, and can I somehow work in my profession during travels? And with all the planning, my excitement started. Because I realised that there are so many things in this world I can learn, and wouldn't be able to do so as easily and quickly if I stayed at home. I started to see a whole new world with lots of opportunities, and I realised I would regret it if I didn't leave my comfort zone and have a closer look at them. I still remember how much freer, and how many more opportunities came my way after the break-up. I had so many ideas and now didn't have to worry that maybe my travel partner wouldn't like them.

This feeling of "actually I could stay in Germany because..." lasted right up until my trip started. So I know how hard it is to actually make the move to leave your comfort zone and dive into the unknown.

After travelling alone for eight weeks, I now really appreciate it. Because you are not alone. This is what you will learn the first day you arrive in a hostel. But the best part of it is that you can choose to be alone if you want.

Of course there are moments when I feel lonely, and don't know what to do, and wish someone would make the decision for me or with me. Those moments come and they make me feel like a little boat out on the open water at night. I realise in these moments that it helps to focus on myself, to accept the feeling of loneliness, and then try to treat myself the best I can. Going to bed early, reading my book, having a nice dinner by myself, etc. I learned that these moments don't last long, maybe just an evening, and the next day the excitement of all the opportunities starts again, and I can do whatever I want.

Emily Chrystie, 29, is from Devon, UK, and currently works as a Location Manager for the HALO Trust in Sri Lanka. She applied after seeing an ad on a job site, started with the organisation in 2017 as an Operations Officer, and completed six months of training in three countries. I met Emily whilst backpacking in South Africa.

I remember my first solo trip as a weekend rough camping on the moors in the UK when I was 18. It seemed something simple to organise at the time, but was a challenge, and made a lasting impact on me. The level of alertness and connection that comes from being totally alone, from sleeping alone, navigating, making decisions without guidance or discussion, is something uncomfortable at first but ultimately invigorating.

Prior to the job I'm doing now, I used to work as a freelance expedition/mountain leader. I worked my way through the British Mountain Leader qualification, and subsequently the International Mountain Leader, and led trips in France, Spain, Italy, Morocco, Egypt and India. In 2015-16 I began to move into humanitarian work, volunteering in a search-and-rescue team on Greek islands where refugees were arriving by boat from Turkey. After this, I trained in humanitarian landmine clearance, a job that has taken me to Cambodia, Abkhazia, Somaliland, Colombia, and to my current role in Sri Lanka, and has allowed me to gain qualifications in Explosive Ordnance Disposal.

I have always been supported by my parents, even if they would prefer that I stick to more politically stable contexts and stop seeking out minefields to visit! I'm lucky enough to have a few close friends who live similar lifestyles and understand that a 'settled' career/lifestyle does not suit everybody. I find these are some of the strongest and most enduring friendships, even if we tend to meet fleetingly on the occasions our travels take us to the same country. Many people are confused by the decision to live 'nomadically', and see it as a phase, or something to "get out of your system". When I was guiding, clients would often ask when I was going to get a "real" job. I always wondered what prompted that question, as guiding is a full-on job with a lot of responsibility. Similarly, now that I work in humanitarian landmine and explosive ordnance disposal, I am often asked if I get paid, or if I am a volunteer. I think this reflects a misunderstanding by many people that travel, regardless of the reason, can only be a frivolous, maybe even meaningless venture. That a 'proper' career and a way of life cannot be built on movement, only on stability.

I used to lead several mountain hiking trips on Corsica. Whilst the main GR20 long-distance trail is well travelled and well marked, there are other fantastic hikes on Corsica that are a lot more remote. Whilst checking out these routes alone prior to taking trips, I remember several occasions where local men would stop me on my way past the last habitations before the mountains, and insist that it was too dangerous for a woman to venture into the mountains alone. As travellers, listening to local advice and warnings is a crucial part of staying safe. However, this is a challenge that has repeated itself for me countless times, in countless countries – the challenge of knowing when well-meaning advice should be followed, and when it is born from an ingrained prejudice that sees women as vulnerable and needing protection, or at risk from nothing more than being alone. This can lead to being advised not to drive, not to walk alone, not to climb, not to cycle, not to swim... the list goes on. The challenge is learning how to tell sensible advice pertaining to the local context from advice that stems from a social understanding of what women, in particular, should or should not attempt alone.

Social structures, public voices and the media are continuously telling us that women are weaker and less able than men. A challenging discovery for me was realising the extent to which I had assumed these stereotypes myself – not just concerning what I considered myself able to do, but also in what I expected of other women. One of the best things about travelling alone, however, is how open you become to meeting others. I've met and gained a deep respect for many men and women in many countries, but a powerful experience for me was how this changed my understanding of how women, specifically, are perceived and treated.

When guiding, I met inspiring women who were clients, colleagues or solo adventurers on the mountain, and began to realise that stereotypes are only as true as we make them. In mine clearance, I have met incredible women who have overcome unimaginable challenges to support their families – female de-miners in Somaliland, who overcame immense societal pressure that restricts women from working, plus huge prejudice against the 'suitability' of women for mine clearance; women in Cambodia and Colombia who are breadwinners for their families, raising their children, whilst working in remote camps doing tough and dangerous work. Travelling alone puts you in a position whereby it is natural to meet others, to share experiences and to learn from each other. I have learnt (and am still learning), just how great the challenges faced by women are in many parts of the world, and in turn feel the privilege of a passport and education that allows me the freedom of movement that is denied to so many.

I think a lot of the level of security experienced whilst travelling alone depends more on the manner in which it is done, rather than the specific country. Whilst some countries are invariably less relaxing to travel in, contextual logistical factors can be just as, if not more important. Do you have a local contact you can call if you need support? Do you have some back-up cash, in case you get stranded? I felt more vulnerable bivying alone at night on the South West Coastal path than I did sleeping in a compound in Somaliland, with the security of an evacuation plan, armed guards and multiple forms of communication to hand.

Travelling in Egypt just after the revolution in 2014, I remember feeling increasingly insecure due to a number of events that culminated in being accosted at knifepoint in broad daylight in Cairo. A friend of a friend put me in touch with someone local who I was able to spend some time with, and by getting to know her and her family, I developed a greater understanding of the local context, and gradually stopped feeling so vulnerable. Travelling without roots or back-up can be exhilarating, but it can also leave you isolated if things go wrong, regardless of the country you are in.

When you arrive somewhere new, connecting with

people – if only a short conversation or friendly greeting – can make a huge difference in terms of support if things go wrong further down the line. Being non-confrontational is also a great help: not just in the physical sense, but in being able to observe and absorb opinions and situations without reacting in a way that may single you out as hostile to certain politics, customs or beliefs.

Finding a job in a country you'd like to explore gives an immediate support group, local contacts, and a way to quickly learn about the local context and security. Plus, travelling after having lived and worked in a country can be far more rewarding than entering and leaving as a tourist. It can be a huge commitment though – maybe start small, visit local areas at the weekend, and see if the joy of learning about somewhere new through your own independence is for you.

I see a nomadic lifestyle as just that – a lifestyle. People often relate travel to holidays or gap years, but in reality it can be a life choice. Just like any other life choice, this means good days, bad days, and average days. Bad things happen just as they do in sedentary lives, but I have never felt targeted solely due to the fact that I'm travelling. The distances involved and lack of secure base can exacerbate the bad – family emergencies far from home, security crises, concerns for personal safety – but also the good – reunions with close friends, learning a new language, or catching a glimpse of your own culture through someone else's eyes.

Mary Foote is 41, lives in New York, USA, and works as an infectious disease physician at the NYC Department of Health and Mental Hygiene. I met Mary in Punta del Este, Uruguay.

Please tell us a little bit about your job and where it has taken you in the world.

I work on emergency preparedness and response for emerging infectious diseases. Unfortunately, since it's a local government position, there isn't much chance to travel internationally (except one trip to Geneva for the bioweapons convention) but I travel domestically several times a year for meetings and conferences. Before this job, I worked in global health (my specialty was TB/HIV), so I got to live and work in several places, including a year in Mysore, India (a research fellowship), one semester in Egypt, a semester in rural Nicaragua, one year in Iquitos, Peru (Amazon region), and lots of shorter trips elsewhere.

What do you love most about travelling?

Variety, seeing new landscapes, meeting folks and learning about different cultures. I especially love the opportunity to get out of my comfort zone and be more social and adventurous. Hiking and good food/wine are also big motivators for where I choose to travel.

What, in your eyes, is the most challenging aspect of travelling as a female?

Depending on where you are, the harassment from men (though probably less of an issue as I get older), and sometimes not being able to travel as freely, due to safety concerns.

And what, if any, are the benefits?

I think women traveling solo are more approachable, so it's easer to meet people. I've also had many fun situations where families have taken me under their wing knowing I'm traveling alone, which has lead to great experiences.

Do you have any places you always go to feel good? Places you could recommend other females travelling to on their own?

Internationally, I don't often go to the same place again, except for Mexico, which is always great, and I do love Portugal and Greece for easy comfortable fabulous trips. In the US, I go to Sedona, northern New Mexico, and Asheville repeatedly, and I never get tired of it.

Do you have any advice for first-time solo travellers? Ways to stay safe, feel less awkward in a restaurant, ways to find company when you

need it, and get out of scrapes when you don't?

I've never been good about being cautious, but definitely ask the locals about safety concerns or anything to be aware of. I'm always hesitant to go alone into people's homes since it can make you feel really vulnerable if something starts to feel uncomfortable, but go with your gut (this varies widely based on where you are). I now always get a local SIM card to have data/phone access, and have someone local or that you meet added into your contacts in case you need quick advice, etc.

If dining alone, I always like to sit at the bar if that's an option, and usually end up striking up a conversation... If not, I always have a book. As I get older I tend to prefer guesthouses/B&Bs, but if I'm keen to meet fellow travellers I'll go with a hostel and take advantage of free city walking tours, as they're a great way to meet people (especially when not at a hostel).

Did you find any particular places more difficult to travel around than others? How did you deal with that?

In general I found parts of North Africa (Morocco and Egypt, in particular) pretty tough as a women due to the crazy intense harassment you can come across, and getting followed a lot was an issue for me. It's always much better if you can find a man to travel with. Some areas of India were pretty intense for that too... the staring can get really uncomfortable! Parts of East Africa I've been in can be a bit harder in terms of getting to more out-of-the-way places and infrequent buses/matatus, and I'm not sure I'd be comfortable driving myself around some of those countries.

What wouldn't you leave home without?
Headlamp! Duct tape, emergency toilet paper, Pepto-Bismol, collapsible water bottle, day pack for hiking.

What have been some of your travelling highlights?
So hard to say since everywhere is special in different ways! I did LOVE the western Balkans... and Georgia (country) more recently. The Costa Alentejo in Portugal was pretty damn magical (these all hit the sweet spot of having great food, hiking and wine).

You've done a lot of travelling on your own, do you travel differently now than when you were in your twenties? What's changed for you?
I tend to stay more at guesthouses/B&Bs, since it's more comfortable and private but still usually intimate enough to meet other people. I still stay at hostels sometimes but

always hesitant to be the "old lady". I'm also much more comfortable renting cars and driving myself now, especially as GPS and navigation programs are so much better and more reliable. Unfortunately, now that I have a real job, I can't travel as much or for as long, which makes me sad, but I try to make the most of the time I do have.

Where would you love to travel to next?
The Pamir Highway in Tajikistan, the Himalayas (Jammu and Kashmir and/or Pakistan, if and when the political situation improves) and New Zealand.

Rachel Harvie, 40, from London, UK, is a self-employed television producer and director. She frequently travels for work, but her heart remains in her childhood home of Cornwall. She has a sociology degree, and has worked her way up from a TV runner to where she is today. I met Rachel whilst studying at Cardiff University.

How old were you when you first went away on your own?

I guess my first real experience of traveling alone was on my gap year, when I taught English in Vietnam. This idea was treated with total confusion and awe from my friends at the time. Vietnam was certainly not on the travellers' map, like it is today, and for many was still associated with the war. My family were great – nervous on my behalf, but I think also impressed that I wasn't off to Australia or Thailand, like the others. I was totally terrified, I'd never done anything like this before, but I definitely had the arrogance of youth!

Coming back was awful, I don't think I was a very nice person. No-one understood me or what I had seen, etc... I remember being reprimanded by my mum for my superior attitude – something that mortifies me now. On reflection, I'm not entirely sure that's what it was. Perhaps just a feeling of being different?

Why do you sometimes travel alone?

I've taken approximately four big trips alone, plus many smaller ones. I guess there is no exclusive reason why I travel alone – self-employment can mean I find myself with sudden time off, and not always someone to go and play with. I can take extended periods away from work – a luxury that many don't have. I'm often single, which means the default option of choosing a partner is not always there. As one gets older, those travel buddies that perhaps existed in your twenties are no longer around. I'm also genuinely happy with my own company, perhaps not for long periods of time, but I don't wish to compromise my desire to travel just because I have no obvious companion.

What do think are the advantages and disadvantages of travelling alone as a woman, and has this changed as you've got older?

Perhaps one of the most distinct advantages is the ability to be totally, utterly and wildly selfish – something that I hope I'm not in real life. If I want to lie on a beach all day and read terrible books, I can. If I want to treat myself to a night in luxury, then there is no-one there to judge. It's also lovely to have total control over your whole journey. Inevitably travels with groups are about compromise, whereas travelling alone allows you to go wherever you wish. There is also the undeniable fact that you can strike up relationships more easily when you are alone, whether with fellow travellers or locals.

I have definitely felt more confident and self-assured travelling alone as I have got older. This is due to there being a broader self confidence, as well as perhaps having more money, and a slight shift in places I choose to go. I think I'm more self aware, more prepared to say no, and just more mindful of any sticky or complex situations I may find myself in.

You often travel to make your television programmes. How has being a woman impacted your ability to do your job in both good and bad ways?

I've travelled a little bit abroad alone for work (such as Ghana), but most of it tends to be in the UK. Generally, with age, I have got much more secure in taking a book to dinner and embracing some alone time, but certainly when I was younger I hated it.

I can work at my own speed, and in my own way, and develop relationships with people in my own right, which are distinct advantages. I can keep my own hours, do my own thing, and come and go as I wish. However, it also means the onus is on me. I have to think, direct and produce everything alone, which ultimately is quite a bit of pressure. It's also arrogant to think that I am always right when telling a story, and much of directing is a true collaborative experience.

How do your family and friends view your decision to travel alone?

My family are all great travellers, and my mum's early travels as a young hippy in Sudan – as well as a more recent resurgence of adventures – have definitely ensured that I felt very supported in my decisions to travel alone.

Perhaps there is one exception to this, which was when I got back from a seven-month stint alone in India. I found this to be a very challenging experience, both due to the emotional upheaval, as well as being in such a culturally different place. It was very hard to articulate this to family, who felt that I should just get on with it. It was only a year later when a series of very high-profile, and truly horrific, rape cases came to light in the country. This sense of sexual vulnerability was a very real feeling while I was there. It was only after the event that my family understood how stressful and anxiety-provoking my adventures must have been.

My younger sisters have travelled a lot for work – supported by a work system, but nonetheless living in risky places, such as Yemen and Myanmar. This means that my mum has had to learn coping mechanisms when we are off gallivanting alone.

I think many friends are jealous of the lack of time limitations I sometimes experience because of work. However, when it comes to travelling alone, this becomes less appealing. Many are not happy for too long in their own company, and perhaps fear they may get bored, or may not know what to do with themselves. They may not have the guts to pack a bag and go, to be impulsive, book a flight and see what happens.

That said, I think in recent years, as many have had children, there are a large number of my female friends who would do anything for some kind of solitary mini-adventure. Time alone without a demanding shadow is but a distant memory. I suspect, on reflection, that most people feel a mixture of emotions when I announce a little time alone – some can't understand it at all! They perhaps perceive it as rash and odd. Deep down, I suspect this is just a bit of old-fashioned envy.

In your opinion, what are the best things about travelling on your own as a female?

I'm sure that I've struck up more friendships, met more people and have had more 'random' experiences as a single woman than I have when in groups or in a couple. I have been invited into more homes, helped out more, been guided and listened to when I've been alone. I feel I look much less approachable in a group setting. This, for me, is wonderfully important. I don't always want to go away to then talk to a whole load of people just like me.

And what are the most challenging?

Being mindful of safety and my own predicament. This is obviously more of an issue in some countries than others. Is it wise to walk into a family home in a mountain village in Morocco? I don't know, but I think it's often worth the risk. I have had very few unpleasant experiences abroad, and probably have many more in Central London over the course of year. It can be tedious to explain that yes, you are alone, and no, it's not the most tragic thing in the world, and yes, you do have friends... Sometimes there is something to be said for just being left alone in peace. I think this is harder when you are often the subject of huge curiosity.

Equally, there are moments when you can feel very,

very alone. During a long period in India, there were days when I did not talk to anyone. It's possible to feel very isolated, or like the rest of the world has somebody.

Travelling alone is also more stressful. I think there is a perception that travelling is always restful, but that is far from the truth. Planning, organising, reading, thinking and plotting all have to be done to ensure you have the best adventure possible, but this takes time, energy, and some serious brain power. Sometimes it's a very attractive option just to shirk this responsibility, but by and large this is impossible when you are alone.

Have there been any particular countries that you've found easier to travel in than others?
I would say Europe is easier, but the downside is that it's more expensive. But it's more familiar, and some enthusiastic language skills can get you a long way.

I was expecting to find Dubai and the surrounding area quite troublesome, but they were actually very welcoming, and much less intimidating than I thought. I attracted a lot of stares, but nothing like the intimidating and unpleasant stuff I received in India.

I loved being in Italy alone. It's a terrible cliché but I was welcomed everywhere I went. I travelled by train, and although I was frequently a subject of fascination, I never felt this was sinister or intimidating. I found myself eating glorious pasta, drinking divine wine in the most wonderful of places. Even in large cities such as Rome and Venice, I was left to my own devices – which actually, in that setting, was exactly what I wanted.

Often it's about those around you being able to read a situation. Sometimes a solitary coffee and a good book are just what you're after. Other times, you're craving a chat. Perhaps there are some places in the world that are just better, or rather more culturally aware of reading those non-verbal cues.

I also had some glorious experiences in Honduras – one of the most dangerous countries in the world. It was truly unexpected! I was quite anxious having left my travel companions of five months. People were eager to help me, point me in the right direction, rip me off occasionally... but broadly speaking, desperate for the tourists to return and spend money.

Any that you've found harder? Why was that?
India I found deeply stressful. I had fled the UK after some heartbreak, and went off for seven months to teach and work and "find myself". I was probably more vulnerable than usual, but overall found it a very challenging country, and I met many women that were leaving prematurely. It's a hard place, especially the

north, as there are no hostels or easy meeting places, so a sense of loneliness can be particularly strong. I would go for days without meeting people. It was also culturally different from anywhere I'd been before. The poverty, politics and general attitude to women left me all at sea, and this contributed to a daily struggle.

I woke up on several occasions on trains and buses to find a man resting his hand on my thigh. It was the supreme confidence of the act that I found surprising. And my response, as a result, was very flustered. I hated myself for not being more robust and assertive; instead, I was embarrassed and self-conscious as I gently moved his hand away. This happened on numerous occasions, and each time it took me by surprise. I have no idea how I could prevent it, bar stay awake for 36 hours!

I was determined to stick at India, but I found it tedious, hard, isolating and, at times, boring. I'm not a quitter, but this took all my energy. I certainly had some unique experiences there, but not something I would repeat alone.

By the time I reached Goa and Kerala, I was much more confident, and indeed it felt like a different country. I could finally relax and enjoy myself.

What advice would you give to anyone who might want to travel alone but is too afraid, too busy, or too skint?

DO IT. I'm hopelessly disorganised, and never know what I'm doing, but with a little forward planning, some thought, and a little confidence, the world can be a wonderful place. I think technology has made travel easier, and the world smaller. I have an app on my phone called Find My Friends. Even small things like that can make any anxious loved ones feel like they're part of your experience.

Hostels and shared living set-ups are the most perfect way to meet people and keep it affordable. I started feeling too old for dorms, but mix it up. Some nights in a room and then others in a dorm can keep you sane.

Any particular things you always take with you that you wouldn't leave home without?

Some lovely products. You can be roughing it, but with some fancy products, life can seem very doable. Make sure you have some good books and reading material. It's often a real luxury having the time to read or think or write, so make the most of it.

Dani Elsdon-Williams is an outdoor adventure guide from New Zealand. We met in Faro, Portugal.

Kia Ora! I'm Dani, a 23-year-old wannabe world traveller. Right now, I'm on my phone in a hostel in Iran drinking chai. My work depends on the season. In the summer, I work as a raft guide. Most recently, I spent four months in Slovenia working on the beautiful turquoise waters of the Soča river. To work in Slovenia I did the Slovenian Whitewater Rescue course, but my rafting qualifications were done with the New Zealand Rafting Association. Sometimes I'll chase the summer, working six months in the Southern Hemisphere, then six months in the North. But last year I decided I missed the snow, and I moved to the Arctic Circle in Finland to teach skiing. I did a Finnish National Association of Snow Sport Instructors course while I was there to get qualified.

What inspired you to work in the outdoor industry, and how did you get started?
I always knew I wanted a job that allowed me to travel. But it wasn't until my last year of high school that I figured out that was possible. I was lucky enough to join a World Challenge expedition that my school was organising. If you don't know, World Challenge is an

organisation that takes a group of students to a developing country to help them build valuable life skills whilst on the adventure of a lifetime.

Our expedition leader was a woman named Dulkara Martig, also a Kiwi. I remember her telling us she couldn't figure out what she should do after our trip. She had to decide between a sea-kayaking expedition in Alaska, a cycle trip down the coast of South America, or a two-week hike deep in the forests of the South Island of New Zealand. I decided right then and there that I wanted to live that life. I wanted the biggest problems in my life to just be deciding on the next big adventure!

From there I did a two-year Diploma in Adventure Tourism in Nelson, New Zealand. In this course, we learnt how to work and guide in most outdoor pursuits. From sea-kayaking and whitewater rafting to skiing, hiking, and even rock climbing. This course is awesome, if you have any interest in working in the outdoors industry, I highly recommend finding something similar. The first year gave us a taster into the world of outdoor adventure, allowing us to choose which pursuit suited us best. For the second year we picked our majors, honed our skills, and got qualified! I picked rafting and skiing, obviously!

What have been some of the challenges doing what you do?

I think the hardest thing is saying goodbye to all the wonderful friends I make around the world. You eat, sleep, and work with the same small group of people for six months. You become like a family, and then at the end of the season you all go your separate ways.

Another challenge is not having any consistency in my life. You're constantly moving around, you never know where you will be a year from now, and if you'll be able to make enough money to buy that next plane ticket.

Tell us about some of the places you've been recently, and what you've been up to the past few months.

My work contract for Slovenia finished in September, and I decided to spend the following months travelling until my new contract starts in Finland in early December. I got a cheap flight with some friends to North Macedonia, and from there we went west into Albania, then down into northern Greece where we went our separate ways. I spent a few days exploring Thessaloniki and the Halkidiki coast by myself. I took an overnight bus to Istanbul, where I meet my friend all the way from New Zealand,

and we started our six-week adventure through Turkey, Georgia, Armenia, and Iran.

I have to fly a lot when I'm travelling for work, and I'm aware that this gives me a bigger carbon footprint. So aside from the initial flight, I have been taking buses, trains, and hitchhiking to get from country to country. Unfortunately, flying is unavoidable for me when moving between jobs and countries, but I've really enjoyed the challenge of doing this trip entirely overland. I will definitely try to do most of my future trips this way.

What do you love most about travelling?

I love the different kinds of people that you meet. From the incredibly friendly locals to the other backpackers with amazing travel stories. I love immersing myself in different cultures around the world. I think it's so important to travel as it changes your perspective of the world, and reminds me how lucky I am to be born in New Zealand.

What are some of the challenges?

It can be a shock to see how different cultures live around the world, especially the undeveloped countries. But the people in these countries are almost always much happier and content than those living in developed countries. It reminds me that we don't need everything to be perfect to be happy.

Have you had any favourite countries you've visited so far?

That's such a hard question! I've loved everywhere I've been so far, but Bovec, Slovenia is seriously amazing, I can't wait to go back and work another summer there. Norway will always hold a special place for me, as it was where I started this adventure. Iran also exceeded my expectations – the people here are incredibly friendly and generous. Of course, I also love New Zealand, that pretty much goes without saying. Extra mentions: the beaches of Albania, the mountain towns in Georgia, and the the pomegranate wine in Armenia! It's impossible to narrow it down to just one.

How would someone follow in your footsteps?

I really recommend finding a course similar to the one I did. That way, you can get a taste of the different pursuits and can get a better idea of which area you want to work in. Otherwise, find a company you want to work for and train with them until they say you're ready to start guiding! Then once you've got some experience, it's so easy to talk to your co-workers and get recommendations of season jobs all around the world.

Do you have any tips for first-time female travellers?

It's easier than you think! If you stay in hostels you always meet like-minded travellers and end up touring around with them. Don't be shy, start up a conversation. You never know how many countless friends you can make! For your first trip, pick a place that's considered very safe, especially for females. I loved Portugal for these exact reasons, it's a popular first choice for women travelling solo. In fact, it's where I met Katie!

What do your family and friends think about your lifestyle?

My parents travel a lot themselves, so they definitely understand why I want to live like this. They always said they would support me in whatever career I chose to take, but I do think they want me to come home more often. Unfortunately, I have been out of touch with a lot of my friends in New Zealand – it's so hard when you're constantly travelling to keep those connections. I really hope when I come back home we can pick up where we left off.

What one thing would you not leave home without?

I always take a tiny sewing kit with me, and it's come in handy so many times! I also always take a small, reusable shopping bag, so I can try to limit my plastic consumption.

Where is next on your list?

I'm crossing the border into Iraqi Kurdistan next week, and from there Finland for the winter! After the season I don't have any concrete plans, but I'm hoping to travel overland through the Stans of Central Asia. I should probably visit my family soon as well. Let's see.

Lori Owen is 33 years old from Toronto, Canada. She currently lives in London, UK, and writes a blog called Wanderlush Travel. I met Lori at the Aviation Festival in London.

Tell us about some of the places you've lived and travelled.

I lived in the UK for one summer in 2011, then in Australia for one year (2017-2018), New Zealand for seven months (2018), and now the UK again on a five-year visa. When I lived in Australia, I did an eight-week road-trip with my then boyfriend. We travelled from Darwin down the west coast, and all the way to Brisbane, hugging the coast the entire way. We rented a station wagon and camped – it was the best travel experience I've ever had! I loved Australia and highly recommend it. It's the perfect country to road-trip in.

I also travelled to Bali, Tokyo and Fiji. Fiji was an absolute dream come true. I went as a solo female traveller and it was an amazing experience. Surprisingly, there are a lot of backpackers in Fiji and I met so many people, which made the experience special. I only spent four days in Tokyo, and it was like nothing I had experienced before. The city is insanely vibrant, different and chaotic, in its own special way. The ramen is delicious, too!

Tell us a little bit about your blog, and what motivated you to start it.

My blog started out as a way to document my travels when I first moved to Australia on a working holiday visa. When I first began, I had no idea what I was doing and it was just on a free Wordpress site without a niche. After returning from living abroad, I decided to take the blog more seriously, and Wanderlush Travel has become a place where I share my stories, as well as tips and posts on the expat life. I want it to be a place for people to come and feel inspired to travel and experience living abroad.

What have been some of your solo travelling highlights so far?

My decision to move abroad to Australia alone turned into my greatest adventure yet. It was the BEST year of my life and it led me to amazing career opportunities, lifelong friends and one amazing road trip. The solo move to Australia then resulted in moving to New Zealand with my then boyfriend and a few other friends from Australia. Amazing memories for life! That experience also fuelled the fire and sparked my love for travel to an undeniable level – and it's just a non-negotiable part of my life now.

What are some of the benefits of travelling solo?

There are so many benefits of travelling alone as a female.

I think it's incredibly empowering, and brings on a huge sense of independence and confidence. Solo travel has helped shaped me more into the woman I want to become. I don't feel the need to rely on others; I can get by and do things on my own. I can be in situations that are quite challenging at times and come out of them stronger than before.

Another huge benefit is not having to rely on anyone to do the things I want to do. You are on your own schedule and can decide where to go, when to go and just whatever you feel like doing in general. It's very liberating!

And what, in your eyes, is the most challenging?
I think the most challenging part is feeling safe and not being taken advantage of. It's a shame to have to feel this way, but there is always a chance of being sexually assaulted or mugged. Another challenge is loneliness. I don't think this is just for women, either – it can happen to anyone who's travelling alone. I sometimes get lonely, but I remind myself why I am doing each trip and really take the time to enjoy my own company.

What would you say to anyone who might think solo travel is selfish?
I really don't think it's selfish at all. In fact, solo travel is a form of self-love in my eyes. It can bring remarkable

experiences to oneself, and help us grow in so many ways that benefit not only us, but our loved ones, and those we encounter in our life as well. It makes us stronger, more patient, more open-minded, independent, able to adapt well to new situations...

the list goes on.

Have your family and friends ever expressed their concern over your decisions, and how have you handled this?

Yes, absolutely. When I first told my family I was making the choice to move to Australia, I was 30, and my mother especially had something to say about it. In a world driven by society's obsession to climb the corporate ladder and buy a house, get married (all the things our parent's grew up knowing), she had a hard time accepting the fact I was throwing away a job at a really great company that could give me a promising future. A promising miserable future, in my mind. I was so unhappy where I worked, and with what I was doing in my life at that point. This was the bold move I had to make to kick my life back into happiness gear and bring back my zest for life.

My mother came around as the trip came closer, and I had to understand that this was not a life she understood, or was used to herself. Now she knows this is the kind of life that brings me happiness and she fully supports my choices.

My best advice would be to explain to your family and friends why you are doing what you do – that it fills you with happiness and lights your fire. Not everyone will agree with your choices. You can't please everyone, but you should be pleasing yourself. You have one life to live. Follow your dreams or you may end up regretting it.

What would you say to other girls who would like to move abroad? Are there any resources you can recommend?

Just do it! Take the leap, it's 100 per cent worth it, and you won't regret it. I was also scared to travel alone for the first time, but after that I became completely addicted. I've heard from people who suffer from anxiety that travel has helped them in amazing ways. It can do wonders for you. You'll be hooked!

I would also suggest researching a lot online, such as blogs, especially those written by female travellers who started the same way. They can be so inspirational. Look on Pinterest for tips and blogs. Join Facebook groups, connect with others on Instagram, and join a Meetup travel group to meet other like-minded travellers – it will help with the fear, and help you find your tribe.

They say your tribe is your vibe.

Facebook is great for finding jobs abroad – there are heaps of groups specifically for backpacker jobs, especially in Australia and New Zealand. Many places also have hospitality job groups and those for au-pairs. Research job sites that are most popular in the country you are going to. For instance, in Australia, www.seek.com.au is very popular, whereas in the UK it's www.indeed.co.uk and **www.reed.co.uk.**

For accommodation, look at Couch Surfing, hostelling, Airbnb, WWOOF, camping, road tripping in a camper van... all these are great options.

Don't be nervous that you are a first-time solo traveller, even the most experienced of travellers started off somewhere, and I think everyone sort of adopts their own way of travel after time – budget travel, adventure, random and spontaneous or luxury travel. For many, solo travel is their thing. And you're never really alone. I always meet like-minded people on the road. You'll be around people more than you think!

One of my favourite things to do is to journal – whether that's sitting on a beach watching the sunset or treating myself to a glass of wine at a local wine bar. Reflecting on my travels and having alone time really helps me connect with myself and express gratitude for the experience. Embrace dining alone – you can really bring all your senses to the meal, and savour all the tastes and aromas. Take in your surroundings and people-watch. I like my own company and enjoy the ambiance of having a wine with dinner – it's slightly romantic, like I am taking myself on a date, and my journaling is like sharing the experience with myself.

To avoid being in bad situations, always be aware of your surroundings and have your wits about you. Don't get wasted if you go out, always tell family members or friends where you are going/staying and you can even share your Uber location with friends. Use your judgement when you meet new people, and trust your gut. Do you get a good feeling or an uneasy feeling? Your gut is always right. Be smart. Being cautious of where you are travelling to and doing research ahead of time is key so you can avoid being in a potentially dangerous area or situation. Anything can happen, but I don't think you should let the fear of solo travel get in the way.

Are there any places you could recommend other females travelling to on their own?

I just ventured to Portugal and absolutely loved it! I fell in love with the country with its gorgeous beaches, laid-back vibes and welcoming people. The south of Portugal on the Algarve coast, and the smaller surf towns were my favourite part. I rented a car for 10 days and did a solo trip. I was nervous to go to Portugal alone and rent a car, but I have never felt so safe in a country and it was quite easy to navigate. The people are warm and gave amazing suggestions on places to visit. I will definitely be back! I would also recommend Australia, Ireland and New Zealand.

How can we travel more responsibly and sustainably in this era of blogging?

I think with the surge in social media, especially Instagram, travel is now at our finger tips, sparking that wanderlust. This has positive and negative impacts. It increases tourism to places, which in turn increases revenue and assists in job creation perhaps, but at the same time the human footprint can be very detrimental for some destinations.

What perhaps were once secret or lesser-known destinations have now become overrun with 'grammers and drones. I think the standard twirling dress on Instagram with a picture-perfect mountain backdrop has ruined travel in some cases, as people flock to these destinations to "get it for the gram" – and we forget to enjoy what the beauty of nature really has to offer.

And yet, I am one of those slightly guilty for this rise of

Insta-travel. I also yearn to get that amazing photo, and I don't see it slowly down among this generation. I think the main thing is to respect the land.

There is a saying I love: "Take nothing but a photograph and leave nothing but a footprint."

What wouldn't you leave home without?

I always bring my reusable water bottle when I travel. I try to reduce plastic consumption as much as possible, and something as simple as taking a water bottle with you can have a huge impact. I also like to bring my journal.

Follow Lori on www.wanderlushtravel.com and on Instagram @Wanderlush_Travel

Jini Reddy is an author and journalist living in London. She's written for *The Guardian*, *BBC Wildlife* and *National Geographic Traveller*, among others. Her book, *Wild Times*, was published by Bloomsbury in 2016, and her new book, *Wanderland*, comes out in April 2020.

Travel is in my DNA. I was born in London, raised in Quebec, Canada, to Indian parents, who were themselves born and raised in South Africa. To not want to travel would have felt quite unnatural to me. Beyond that, when I was growing up I'd read about men doing adventurous things, and wished I could troop across the desert or whatever. I never saw anyone who looked like me doing these things – perish the thought of a female adventurer featured in any books or on TV, never mind a woman of colour – but it never occurred to me that I could *not* embark on adventures of my own. It was just a question of figuring out how. I can't deny that it would have been so much easier, and infinitely more confidence-boosting had I had role models who looked like me, though.

Tell us about your first solo trip, and what drew you to a life of travel and adventure.
My very first solo trip was aged 13, when my parents put me on the plane to visit my sister, then living in the

Scottish Highlands. When I was a university student in Canada, I went backpacking in Europe. It was a kind of rite of passage. But my first proper big solo trip was to Nepal. I was in my twenties, I'd quit my job, had a one-way ticket, no credit card and £500. I had no phone either, for this was all pre-internet/pre-mobile phone days.

I had vague plans to volunteer, but that fell through, so instead, after a nerve-wracking first 24 hours, I gathered my wits and resolved to go trekking on the 21-day Annapurna Circuit, without sherpa or group, never having done more than a walk in the Peak District before. I was quite naïve. Fortunately, I met a guy from Yorkshire on the bus to the trailhead and ended up hiking with him. The company came in handy when crossing a 5,500-metre pass, which was far, far tougher than I had imagined. I had a bad case of altitude sickness, was throwing up constantly, and had to bed down in a goat herder's hut on the other side as I was too weak to carry on to the next village.

But I can still remember so much of that trip: it gave me my travel legs, so to speak. And it was a further two years before I eventually returned to Britain, not without regret.

What's been your experience of travelling solo as a woman of colour?

Mixed, and interesting. In Europe, I am far more conspicuous, hyper-visible in some places. Which means I choose where I go with care. I pay attention to the news and current affairs. There are still few women of colour writing on travel, at least where features are concerned, so, ironically, I can't rely on a travel feature to let me know if a place is 'safe' for me. I don't want to end up somewhere where I likely won't be welcome. That wouldn't be any fun. The flip side is that, in India for instance, being Asian, I'm invisible. Which is quite freeing, but also disconcerting as I'm so unused to it. But in many places, particularly in the Global South, I feel there is a level of trust and warmth that is there from the outset, which otherwise might not be. I'm generalising – it's not the case everywhere – but I often feel that I am welcomed in as 'one of us'. That is a very nice feeling.

Please tell us a little bit about your work, what it's about, and where it has taken you in the world.

Journalism was my second career – my first was in book publishing, on the editorial side. As a travel writer, I was in at the deep end from the start, visiting Japan and Kyrgyzstan within the space of three weeks! I could hardly believe my luck. My byline has appeared in a wide variety of national newspapers and magazines in the UK, but the more I travelled, the more I began to be drawn to natural, wild landscapes, and to people from indigenous cultures. I found their reciprocal, intimate way of connecting with the natural world enchanting. My interest grew and I began to segue into writing about nature and landscape.

My new book, Wonderland, is out in April 2020, and it's about my journey to connect with the magical in the landscape, in Britain. I wanted to know what it might be like to commune with the land in a way less ordinary. Instead of a map, might it be possible to plot a journey by asking the spirit of the land to guide me? What might unfold if I were to do this? It's a bit whimsical but I loved researching it. There are elements of memoir in the book too. My first, *Wild Times,* a hybrid guidebook/narrative on a nature and connection theme, was published in 2016 and won the book prize at the British Guild of Travel Writers the following year.

You write a lot about nature and the natural world. Do you have any favourite places that make you feel good?

Canada, always – half my heart is there. There is a particular stretch of the St Lawrence River, in Montreal, that feels like heaven to me. In the UK, locally in London,

Wimbledon Common and the Richmond riverfront. Otherwise: Lindisfarne's North Shore; Bryher Island, in the Isles of Scilly; a stretch of coast on Portland, in Dorset; stretches of the South West Coast path. Further afield, parts of New Zealand and Namibia. In both places, I have had a sense of nature being unfettered, sovereign even, and at ease with itself.

Do you have any tips and advice for first-timers?

Accept that you will feel some anxiety – that is a part of it. Trust that it will dissolve once you get going. Learn about the culture and the customs of the place you are travelling to, particularly if further afield, and practice some phrases in the local language, or one of the local languages. Be respectful. If you're in a conservative country, dress modestly. Be kind, smile. Equally be alert. Don't do anything you wouldn't do at home. Watch and see what the locals do. Always, always listen to your intuition. If something doesn't feel right, it probably isn't.

Also, take small steps. If you want to hike alone in the UK, try a day-long coastal walk first. You can't get lost with the sea in your sights! Wear boots with ankle support, take a walking stick, ample water, snacks, waterproofs and a map.

In terms of finding company, in cities or towns I find that happens naturally once I let go off the intense need to find company. (There's a great lesson in that.) Otherwise, you could sign up for one of the many group tours run by local guides, where you will meet fellow travellers. Day-long group tours, focused on food and drink or some specialist theme, can be fun. Longer group tours are more of a commitment, and it's pot luck who your travel companions will be, but they're handy if you're travelling to remote places, where independent travel isn't always possible, or you don't have months and months for an extended journey.

If I'm in a restaurant alone, I'll take a book, drink a glass of wine, find a corner seat, scribble notes. All help, though I can't pretend there haven't been moments, particularly in places that are very family-oriented, or in cultures where women don't tend to dine out alone, when I've scarfed down my food and scuttled back to my lodgings. I once had to write about a Mumbai nightclub. I can tell you it was with gritted teeth that I walked in on my own. I glued myself to the bar, had a drink and made small talk with two very polite, slightly bemused men, checked my watch and then waltzed out of there. I'd lasted all of 45 minutes.

Hostels are good too, if you're hiking alone and don't mind roughing it, as they have communal spaces. Some even have private rooms so you get the best of both worlds. Bus and train rides are also excellent ways of meeting locals and fellow travellers alike. But often I really enjoy my own company, especially when in the countryside or out in nature. Hiking alone is my idea of heaven – course that's easier and safer in some parts of the world than others. If hostels aren't your bag, and you don't feel like schlepping your tent around, you could try staying in a bothy. In the UK, the National Trust have some lovely (lockable) bothies. I remember a beautiful couple of nights in one on Exmoor.

So far I have never really found myself in a scrape. There is an element of luck in that. On late-night buses in India at times I have felt uneasy – particularly when border guards have got on to check my passport – but generally speaking, I'm quite clear about my boundaries. I don't engage in small talk out of politeness if I am feeling uncomfortable.

How has travel changed you as a person?
It has empowered me, given me a more interesting life, made me more aware that there is more than one way of living, thinking, and doing things. It has deepened my feelings of empathy and compassion towards the plight of refugees, and given me greater understanding of the

sacrifices they have made. Travel has made me more aware of the extraordinary richness of our world. It has also made me eager to help when I see a tourist looking bewildered. I am so grateful for the experiences I have had.

Can you share some of your travelling highlights?

So many! The incredible landscapes in and en-route to Pakistan's North West Frontier Province. Pakistan generally. The warmth of the women in Iran. The vastness of the wilderness in Namibia. Learning about Maori culture in New Zealand. Volunteering at Mother Teresa's in Calcutta one Christmas when she was still alive. Fasting and wild camping alone for five nights on a mountaintop in the Pyrenees. Learning to use a compass for the first time on an extended solo hike through Slovenia to Italy. Walking amidst the Living Root Bridges in India – they're the Taj Mahal of the natural world. And Iceland. Woah. I stayed in one of the most remote villages on a fjord in the east coast, and the peace took on a character of its own. It was like a living, sentient being.

What are your thoughts on travel and climate change?

We all need to reduce our carbon footprint. That's a

given. But I don't believe in flight-shaming. If you have family on the other side of the world, and if you have a deep connection to a place that is far away, are you meant to just sever it? Cut off that part of yourself, which may also be connected to your identity? And what about the positives – the understanding and tolerance that comes from exploring further afield? It's not so simple is it?

I think the best thing we can do is to limit the number of flights we take. Travel judiciously. Travel responsibly. Plant trees to offset. Consider who you are empowering with your travel pound. When abroad, stay in places that are locally owned and run, and by people who also care about protecting the planet – they may live in a part of the world that has been deforested or polluted, or has suffered socially and economically, thanks to the greed of industrialised nations.

Spend more time holidaying in the UK. There is so much to explore here, and we have such an extensive network of trains. Take the train if you're travelling in Europe, and make that part of the journey. Cycling holidays can be great fun too. I once cycled the Petit Tour de Manche from Dorset to Brittany, a nine-day journey, with a guide – just the two of us – and I really enjoyed it (bar the steep hills!).

Where was your last big trip and what did you enjoy about it?

My last big trip was to New Zealand. Great Barrier Island, an off-grid, solar power island stole my heart. I also resonated deeply with aspects of Maori culture – the respect and love and feelings of communion with nature. There is so much awe-inducing natural beauty in the country, from North to South. I loved it. I don't know what it is like to live there, but for a humble visitor, it ticked a lot of boxes. And Jacinda Ardern, the current Prime Minister, is so sane! I wish it wasn't so far away. I wish I didn't feel so guilty about my carbon footprint. But there you go. Such is the dilemma of living in the midst of a climate crisis.

Where's next on your bucket list?

Aside from Canada, which I miss, I much prefer exploring the UK these days. I don't really have a bucket list as such. I'm not really one for bucket lists. I'm increasingly exhausted by airports. They're stressful and overcrowded. That said, I have an idea for a new book, and some roaming may be involved. I'm in two minds, as I'd need to take a few flights. Again, I'm torn and racked with guilt at the prospect.

What wouldn't you leave home without?

A talisman. I always carry one with me.

Follow Jini on Twitter: @Jini_Reddy and Instagram: @jinireddy20

Pypa Wait is 26 is from Hampshire, UK, and currently works as a hostess at a restaurant in South Lake Tahoe, California. I met Pypa in Cape Town, after she hitchhiked all the way there from Egypt.

I first travelled alone abroad when I was 18 years old. I had already started travelling/hitchhiking around my small portion of England by the time I was 16, predominantly between the South West and London, but at 18 I, having lost faith in the course I was studying, left the college I was at and flew to Egypt. I spent a short spell, just less than two months, travelling alone through Egypt, Jordan and Turkey, satiating my fascination with ancient/classical cultures, and overwhelming my senses with the modern society existing within those borders. I hadn't the thought to hitchhike there yet, that would come the following year, so I travelled by bus and by boat. It was... exceptional. Challenging. Initiatory and eye-opening.

The day I flew into Cairo (2012) there were still tanks in the street from recent riots. On buses we were stopped and had automatic rifles shoved and shaken in our faces. My first night in Cairo I went out exploring and was followed three times, once so close I could feel his breath on the back of my neck, and he followed me back to the door of the place I was staying. It was affronting and confusing and shook me, but did nothing to dampen my spirit of discovery.

Aside from the being-followed aspect, I loved it. I loved every damn part of it. I loved the smell of steaming desert cities on cool mornings. I loved the scents and colours of cultures I had never encountered that I would subsequently fall ferociously in love with. I loved the sounds of Arabic, Turkish, Persian, Hebrew, falling around my cheeks and over my ears. I loved how hard it was, stretching my patience and challenging me to grow. It struck a match to a fire that had been waiting inside to be lit. I returned to England to earn some money, and when I was 19 I left for good. This juggernaut of experience, this romance I have shared with the world, has guided and shaped my life in every way since then.

My father is an archeologist and during my youth travelled often and for long stretches. My maternal grandparents spent large swathes of their young parenthood in various stretches of the world on account of my grandfather's job: my mother and aunt were born in Kenya; my uncle in Chile; they spent time in Trinidad and Tobago; several years in Nigeria... Following my lineage back further, various great-grandfathers-grandfathers were merchant vessel captains, sailing from

Scotland to and around the Americas. I expect this insatiable curiosity for other worlds is somewhat in my blood, if such things can be so. Regardless, I was brought up on stories of far-flung lands and ridiculous antics (a family favourite is when they made strawberry jam on the side of an erupting volcano, a nod to the undeterrable force that was my grandmother.) What child is not caught by such fancy?

I found out later that my parents were none-too-thrilled to hear I had decided to go to Egypt in 2012, the Arab Spring Uprising still in full force during that time. In 2013, when I left for good at the age of 19 and turned up a year later in South Africa, having hitchhiked alone the distance between, I told my parents initially I was going to work on a farm in Belgium and would likely be back in 2-4 weeks. It wasn't a lie, per se – I truly was to be working on a farm in Belgium, and had no set plans of what would come next. I would be, however, avoiding truth if I didn't admit I indulged in the freedom of semantics. I hadn't any real plans to return soon. I never told them I hitchhiked by means of travel (my only means of travel) nor did I tell them where/when I was en route.

They spent the majority of that year, on account a well-meaning but still outright lie, under the impression that I was somewhere between Ukraine and Greece working on farms. I didn't want to cause any unnecessary stress (I having a mother prone to extreme worry), and nor did I want to tempt them to hunt me down and drag me back, kicking and screaming. There was also another reason; my parents and I... we've had a rough go of it. Who hasn't? Doing this alone – alone of their opinion, alone of outside aid, alone of any stricture or structure imposed by another – was essential to me, though at the time I didn't know why. It was an initiatory passage, and essential to my becoming. So, I Skyped my parents when I was CouchSurfing in Johannesburg, and told them I had spent the last year hitchhiking there from Belgium. I figured that way they couldn't be too worried, it being already done and all.

In the time since then I have hitchhiked through almost 40 countries, which is still far too few in my opinion. The kindness I have encountered has changed my life. No, my apologies, that's a wild under-exaggeration: it has saved my life. The generosity I have witnessed, the compassion I have been shown, the love I have received and given through these interactions has become the cornerstone of who I am as a human being and how I view the world around me. I cannot sing its praises high enough. I have fallen in love in these times. I have driven for days with an individual, and learnt more about the fabric of their being than I have in years of peerhood. I have looked after their children, I have remained in contact years later. I have attended their weddings.

I still remember every ride I took during that time. I still remember the things I spoke about with those people. I remember the pictures of their children they showed me, I remember the medical conditions they were being treated for, I remember being told of one's imminent divorce, one's passion for mending old books, and I remember the way they smelt. I have always been fascinated by the human heart, utterly beguiled by its loves and hates, its habits and discrepancies. The way it behaves in kindness, the way it behaves in pain. The psychology that governs its way of moving through the world.

I love to listen and understand. I was not prepared for how open people would become when faced with a non-threatening presence (me) in a place they felt safe (their car) when they knew they would never see me again. I became as if their therapist, their world spilling out to me, and I felt honoured to hear it. It is such an unusual situation to meet another within... Human to human, we take time to trust one another, years to open up to the point where we can speak freely without fear of judgement. I, being a momentary passer-through, and one who had at that time experienced enough struggle to be a compassionate presence, found myself to be the non-judgemental ear those people so desperately needed. We all need to be heard. We all need to feel there has been at least one person who could hear our story and be a part of its holding, even just for a moment. What an honour to be that person. What an honour to hear the stories these humans carried; their pains and struggle, loves and dreams. The beauty of the human heart astonishes me.

There is something immensely soothing about it. For me, perhaps it's my type of personality or ego, I find motion to be innately soothing. I am never more present than when I am hitchhiking, in part because it's imperative for my safety, but also for the honour of being so completely present with another human. I don't want to miss a moment. I have no idea where we will be next, what will be said next, what will happen next down this road, so I sit, and I pay attention to it all. I liken it to flow state, akin to meditation. Being in that state with another is like magic: time slows, my senses are heightened, I remember the smallest of details. I feel completely comfortable and at home in my skin, my intuition speaking clearly and guiding me forward. It's extremely hard to explain, but I feel more myself than in almost any other situation. In my element.

There is also the matter of trust. There is something about entering into a contract with another that balances delicately on the knowledge that I am almost entirely at their mercy. An unspoken understanding: I give over my safety and place it in your hands. That vulnerability, that trust that is palpable between myself and my companions is uniquely dependent on there being no monetary exchange, and I didn't realise how important that was until I was deeply immersed within it and watching its repercussions. It is a bond formed, and in 99.9999% of instances, it is honoured. It feels like an invitation. "Here, come. Meet me in this place." Watching a person unfold within this space, give when they had not expected to give, care when they had not expected to care... sometimes I think we humans are just waiting for an opportunity to rise, waiting for a chance to be the person we believe ourselves to be capable of. To give selflessly. To give wholly with no presumption of return. I am of the belief I have seen what we have the potential as a race to be, and in that witnessing I saw great love.

The world caught me softly in the palm of its hands and showed me compassion beyond that which words can express. I have been left in awe of humanity. It brings me to tears each and every time I think on it. I am brought to tears as I write this, and each drop is birthed from joy. When I say it saved my life, I mean it with every fibre of my being. Travelling... the people I have met... the way I have been treated... it has been my salvation. It has broken and healed my heart in exactly the same instant time and time again, and witnessing, simply *witnessing* humans and their rich tapestry of existence has been the greatest honour of my life. Despite the struggles of the world, despite the pain and war and heartache, even despite the horrible things that have happened to me during my life and travels, for happen they have, I believe humanity to be good. For I have seen it. I have seen it.

Freedom. That is what travelling alone is for me. Freedom and challenge, both inextricably intertwined, and the only two travel companions I need. I am bound by no other's fears, phobias or close-heartedness, only my own, and these I seek to challenge at every opportunity I can. It forces me to engage, constantly and unwaveringly. When travelling with others, a safety net is always ready to fall back upon – don't want to talk to new people? Don't want to talk in another language? Don't want to ask for directions, order food, talk philosophy or politics? You don't have to. You can discuss them with your friends and remain happily reclined within your comfort zone.

Travelling alone forces you to lean in: lean into the discomfort, lean into the challenge, lean into the unknown and push yourself out of your comfort zone again and again. It can feel relentless at times, but it leads to the most extraordinary of experiences. The calibre of humanity I have met, and the kindness I have encountered due to the fact I had no choice but to thrust myself into their path, has entirely seduced my heart and I am in love. Aside from that, I am free to my own whims, and can engage when I desire, and rest and recover when I am in need.

I don't tend to find countries harder or easier to travel in, except when it comes to language. Obviously in Europe, where English is a common second tongue for many, and particularly the youth, getting around is significantly easier than, say, Panama, while my Spanish is still in its linguistic infancy. Other than that, people are people the world over, governed by the same drives, desires, instincts. I have been cared for beyond comprehension in every country I have visited.

I have friends who have hated travelling alone, and swear they will never do it again. I have travelled alone since the beginning, aside from three weeks in Ecuador with a small group, and I subsequently swore I would never do *that* again! Ha!

The most challenging aspect of travelling as a woman alone is, of course, our sex. Misogyny exists the world over, and though some locations are more inclined to it than others, it is restricted by no border, culture or creed. It can be exhausting – being constantly aware, on guard, on watch – particularly when alone. But for me this is a small price to pay for freedom, which I choose to claim unremittingly, irrespective.

On a more practical note, as a hitchhiker I am aware of the danger I may be exposing myself to and I think it imperative to be aware of my surroundings at all times. I can look after myself, and I trust my gut intuition, but I do not necessarily trust another to be as aware I am, potentially acting in ways that may endanger both them and myself. It is too risky a situation to travel with another who cannot handle themselves, their reactions, or their surroundings.

As I previously mentioned, misogyny and patriarchal dominance is a global phenomenon, but it would be amiss to say it wasn't more blatant in some areas than others. I am disinclined to name, as everyone experiences a place differently, but let it be said that one's watchful eyes are in greater use in various geographical locations.

When taking into account the nature of my travels, one cannot be surprised at some point I would come to heads with an adverse experience. I have punched people, I have kicked people, I have had my hands on both the emergency brake and the door handle and been screaming like a devil-child, but surprisingly the particular event I have in mind didn't happen around hitchhiking. It was simply a moment of innocuous naivety and a dramatic, unforeseen change in cultures that I didn't acclimatise to in time.

The bad things witnessed or acted against us, unless

addressed and processed, inevitably lead to either internal conflict or cognitive dissonance, and it's something I've often considered. Considering how late the hour of our own Western sexual revolution and rise of feminism/female empowerment, can we really assume a place outside of our sphere should adhere to the same belief systems?

Travel and humility has taught me to honour and respect the beliefs of others, even if I don't agree with them, and this doesn't mean I only honour "the good". It means I must also honour what I deem "the bad". I do not believe we can pick and choose the boundaries of compassion; it is either omnipresent, or it does not exist.

That does not mean I support the behaviours of other cultures, but the conclusion I often come to is this: I must meet this in compassion. It is my personal response and I don't expect others to do the same, but my understanding leads to compassion, and compassion to openness, and from this openness I believe we create the meeting place where real change can take place.

Invest in some good self-defence classes before you go, because everyone should know how to break a grip, and it'll come in handy more than once. If you're uncertain, travel in a group for a while as you find your feet then venture out as your confidence grows. Trust. Trust, but be aware.

Travel in groups in strange, new cities, or if there is political tension in the region. Tensions in the higher-ups means tensions in the lower-downs, and things can get a little dicey if the community feels under threat. Travel in groups at night. If you want, take mace, have it to hand and know how to use it. Don't mace yourself. Have someone who knows where you are, where you're going and where you'll be next, and if possible someone that's expecting you.

One thing I *always* do, even if I'm out in the city with only a small backpack, is have a spare scarf and shirt in my pack. It's a quick, easy costume-change, and if you have a very persistent follower it pays to have something to throw them off the scent. I've used this on multiple occasions and it's particularly useful in large crowds or Islamic countries where you'll blend right in with a quick cover-up.

Personally, violence is always a last resort, but I'm a 5ft 2in woman, so preparing to use other means of defence is (one would hope) common sense. I've learnt that it's almost always possible to talk yourself out of an altercation without having to resort to physicality. Learn to desexualise yourself. I cannot stress enough the importance of being aware of your own sexuality and how it displays itself. It's hard to explain, and my theatre background definitely serves me well, but if you're being treated inappropriately by a man, change the way you're perceived. I've deterred the advances of many an older man by carefully moving from a sexualised object to an "individual in need of protection" by an "*honourable* stranger."

If you think you're in danger of being assaulted on the street, or you're being followed by someone you can't shake off, I'm a big fan of starting to hack up my lungs like the Black Death resides within and the plague has me on the brink of collapse. Maybe I spit on the ground a little, too. Drool is optional. No-one has yet to approach me after that show. I remain unmugged.

As stated before, know how to break a grip. Often that's enough. Depending on where you are, pulling at your arm might just be the cultural way of grabbing your attention and nothing further is needed. If someone casually grabs you sexually in a public place, just smack them away and change location or move into a crowd. Infuriating as it is, making a scene rarely helps, but giving them some good ol' crazy eyes can. If you want, know how to land a punch. Use it sparingly, and only if you're sure any resultant fallout can be handled; violence escalates quickly, and particularly if you've bruised an ego by a sexual rebuttal. I recommend against it unless absolutely necessary.

And take a sewing kit! Everything will break.

Everything will break/rip/tear/disintegrate sooner or later. Duct tape is also worth having around. Superglue is an essential. Rehydration tablets/salts, and emergency water purifiers. Also a roll of readily accessible toilet paper. I will repeat myself: You will get the shits.

This is such an astonishing time to be alive. This generation is the first to know a global community of this kind. We can communicate in the blink of an eye with someone 10,000 miles away. We can forge a connection with people we have never met, that we might never meet, but share a fellow cause and offer our support. We can raise awareness of a need that lies somewhere we have never visited, and rally together to send aid. We have an international voice. We can finally, finally make a difference. We are all active members in this earth-encompassing neighbourhood, and the opportunity lies both figuratively and literally at our fingertips.

And yet we stand on the brink of self-annihilation, both at the hands of our polarising leaders and in the wake of our careless exploitation of this inexplicably beautiful planet. As has been said many times before by those wiser than I, *our house is burning*. The West Coast, the Congo, the Amazon. In the political sphere a resurgence grows of divisive propaganda and pomp that calls back from near-extinction the same old themes of Naziism, xenophobia and racism that I think many of us hoped would never again see the light of day. We balance tentatively in between unprecedented potential, and obliteration.

There is a lot of uncertainty in the world and we are still only human. When faced with the unknown, we oftentimes respond in fear. In fear, we build walls and detain children, in fear, we extract ourselves from our allies, in fear we raise barriers to refugees, deaf to their voices that tell us it is because of fear they flee. We find ourselves entrenched within uncertainty, and while the potential for a global community offers itself to us in ways it never has before, we build around ourselves a cage, and sit within.

I find myself mildly bemused when our generation is mocked and discouraged by those of an older age for our tendency to hoist anchor and unravel the sails. I do not think it is a coincidence that the availability and popularity of international travel comes in the same instance as our desperate need for it. I do not think it is a luxury. I think it is imperative.

The only way to a world beyond fear and estrangement, I believe, is understanding, and what better way to understand than to go, and to listen. To *really listen*, and be willing to hear with an open mind and compassionate heart. To immerse oneself in the world of another, to see their humanity and feel it to be the same as your own, to see blood for blood and skin for skin and bone for bone, and recognise deep in one's heart, *we are the same*. We love the same, we suffer the same. These people are our family. Their cause is our cause. Their home is our home. Their humanity is our humanity, and we must give to them the same respect we give to our own. They are the kith to our kin.

This, to me, is the most important aspect of travel. Unity, respect, appreciation.

And now I'll answer in the psycho-spiritual sense, as that's the lens through which my mind's-eye seems to frame the world. It could be called many things: 'Surrender', 'Letting Go', 'Release', but I think I'll choose this:

Unfolding.

The unfolding of the self.

Travel has this extraordinary capacity to both be an act of leaving, and of coming home. Like all the best things in life, and most truisms, it is a paradox.

The coming home of the Self. The remembrance of who one is, one's place within this telluric organism, and the resultant wonder of this great trick-of-the-light we call Life. That alone causes ripples that wash up against the shore of our individual and collective humanity, and I think it to be the most astonishing miracle of all.

It's a strange axiom that stagnation makes us feel

further from ourselves, and it is in the act of wandering that we find our way back. It is not the way for everybody, but for a certain few of us, the further we go, the closer we become, until one day you're walking down a dusty African road, and in a swirl of sight-obscuring smut, you look down at your smeared self in this orange-coloured cloud and realise, "Here I am... Here I am."

Conclusion

Just do it

_____

"Traveling is like flirting with life. It's like saying, 'I would stay and love you, but I have to go; this is my station.'" – Lisa St Aubin de Terán

So this is almost the end of our journey. I hope it's inspired you to get out there ASAP. It's my experience that the world is a much kinder, safer place than we're lead to believe. I, for one, am constantly amazed how friendly and helpful most people are. Most people are good people, and most trips are trouble-free. That's not to say you can trust everyone all of the time – you need to take care of yourself and be informed – but there's a way of doing that judiciously, without scaring yourself half to death and ingesting toxic news that warps your perception of humanity. There will always be bad things happening in this world, and there will always be naysayers. But it's up to us how we react to it all.

Try not to let fear-mongering – and there is a lot of fear-mongering – stop you from seeing the world and getting out of your comfort zone, even if you're not very confident doing so, or are suffering from depression or anxiety. Possibly the best cure for all those things is to get out there and expand your horizons. We are far more adaptable and capable creatures than we are given credit for, or that we give ourselves credit for.

Either way, I think it's far scarier growing old knowing you didn't do all the things you wanted to do while you were young, healthy and fit enough (because you're never as young as you are today, right?). Most of the time, common sense and instincts will prevail, and be ample ammunition to keep you safe and get you out of a tight fix.

The world really is a beautiful place, full of possibility and wonder, and you're missing out if you don't explore as much of it as you can while you're here. We have such a short time whizzing about on this rock. Grab it with both hands and squeeze it hard. And send me a postcard!

Bon voyage.

Where can I go for more inspiration?

―――――――――――

These days, it's easier for us to travel and connect with each other than ever before. There are apps, Facebook groups, forums, Meet Ups, influencers, bloggers and YouTube stars to watch, film festivals to go to, blog to read, and Instagram accounts to salivate over. It now feels more possible than ever before.

Here are a few names to follow to get you in the mood:

1. Travel BFF
2. The Girl Outdoors
3. I Am Aileen
4. Where's Mollie?
5. The Blog Abroad
6. Spirited Pursuit
7. Grrrl Traveler

8. Hey Nadine

9. See Her Travel

10. World of Wanderlust

11. A La Jode

12. Adventurous Kate

13. We Are Travel Girls

14. She Is Not Lost

15. Dame Traveler

16. Dames Travellers

17. Girl Around World

18. Ladies What Travellers

19. Girls Dream Travel

20. Journeys of Girls

21. The Blonde Abroad

22. Be My Travel Muse

23. World of Wanderlust

24. The Sweet Wanderlust

25. Young Adventuress

26. Alex in Wanderland

27. Women on the Road

28. WorldPackers.com

29. Heart My Backpack

Resources

Some films about female travel:

1. Thelma and Louise

2. Wild

3. Eat Pray Love

4. A Private War

5. Shirley Valentine

6. Before Sunset

7. Gorillas in the Mist

8. A Journey Across All Seven Continents by Jacqui Bell

9. A Grand Journey by Kira Brazinski

10. Pacific Lines by Angie Scarth-Johnson

11. Rainbow Dive by Rhiannan Iffland

Also check out the Women's Adventure Film Tour at www.womensadventurefilmtour.com

Books about female travel:

1. *What I Was Doing While You Were Breeding* by Kristin Newman

2. *Wild* by Cheryl Strayed

3. *Extreme Sleeps* by Phoebe Smith

4. *Eat, Pray, Love* by Elizabeth Gilbert

5. *How Not to Travel the World* by Lauren Juliff

6. *Women Travellers*, edited by Mary Morris

7. *Work Your Way Around the World* by Susan Griffith

8. *Wild Times* by Jini Reddy

9. *Departures* by Anna Hart

10. *The Girl Who Climbed Everest* by Bonita Norris

11. *Travels in a Thin Country* by Sara Wheeler

12. *Terra Incognita* by Sara Wheeler

13. *One Woman Walks Wales* by Ursula Martin

14. *A Journal of a Few Months' Residence in Portugal* by Dorothy Wordsworth (1847)

15. *An Octopus in My Ouzo* by Jennifer Barclay

Some good companies to check out for group travel:

1. Explore (explore.co.uk)
2. Exodus (exodus.co.uk)
3. Responsible Travel (responsibletravel.com)
4. Intrepid (intrepidtravel.com)
5. Wild Frontiers (wildfrontierstravel.com)
6. Journey Latin America (journeylatinamerica.co.uk)
7. Solos Holidays (solosholidays.co.uk)
8. Friendship Travel (friendshiptravel.com)
9. Solitair Holidays (singlesholidays.com)
10. Travel One (travelone.co.uk)
11. Small Families (smallfamilies.co.uk)
12. Jules Verne (vjv.com)
13. Flash Pack (flashpack.com)
14. Fixers (fixersworld.com)
15. Health & Fitness Travel (healthandfitnesstravel.com)
16. Chicks on Waves (chicksonwaves.com)
17. Lodged Out (lodgedout.com)

Cheat sheet for ordering a decent bottle of wine in a restaurant. All these are a good bet.

1. Tokaj from Slovakia (stunning and unusual though hard to find)
2. Sancerre from France (predictably good white wine)
3. Surrey Gold (fruity and drinkable white from Denbies, England)
4. Any bacchus grape from England is a decent bet
5. Chapel Down and Camel Valley English wines
6. Nyetimber and Ridgeview sparkling wines from England
7. Pouilly-Fumé and Pouilly-Fuissé from France (both reliable French whites)
8. Malbec from Argentina (classic red)
9. Chenin blanc from South Africa (easy-to-pair white)
10. Pinotage from South Africa
11. Whispering Angel rosé (very drinkable)
12. Vinho verde from Portugal (refreshing for a hot day)
13. Chocolate block from South Africa (expensive but worth it)
14. Quinta do Portal rosé from Portugal
15. Terra Franca from Portugal (very drinkable red)

16. Antão Vaz from Portugal (gorgeous grape variety)
17. Frankovka from Slovakia
18. Chasselas from Switzerland
19. Rebula from Slovenia
20. Movia wines from Slovenia (excellent wine label)
21. Late harvest wines from Washington or Portugal (you can't go wrong with any of them)
22. Sauternes dessert wine (a sure bet)

Some podcasts to listen to while you're on the road:

1. Desert Island Discs by the BBC
2. TED Radio Hour by NPR
3. How I Built This by NPR
4. Where Are You Going? With Catherine Carr, by the BBC
5. Oprah's SuperSoul Conversations
6. Making Sense with Sam Harris
7. Great Escape Radio with Lori Allen
8. Hidden Brain by NPR
9. A History of the World in 100 Objects by BBC
10. The Tim Ferris Show
11. The Guilty Feminist with Deborah Frances-White

Thanks and acknowledgements

Huge thanks to the following people for their
contributions and help:

Emily Chrystie, Pypa Wait, Mary Foote, Lam Duong,
Lori Owen, Dani Elsdon-Williams, Jini Reddy, Rachel
Harvie, Sarah Batterbury, Camilla Simson.

NOTES & IDEAS

Manufactured by Amazon.ca
Bolton, ON